Change, Choices, and Consequences:

A Guide to Mega T'
and

Roger Kaufman, Ph.D., CPT

HRD Press, Inc. • Amherst • Massachusetts
ISPI • Silver Spring • Maryland

Volume I of the *Defining and Delivering Successful Professional Practice—HPT in Action* series

Series Editors:

Roger Kaufman, Ph.D., CPT
Dale Brethower, Ph.D.
Richard Gerson, Ph.D., CPT

Published by:

HRD Press, Inc.
22 Amherst Road
Amherst, MA 01002
800-822-2801 (U.S. and
 Canada)
413-253-3488
413-253-3490 (fax)
www.hrdpress.com

International Society for
 Performance Improvement
1400 Spring Street
Suite 260
Silver Spring, MD 20910
301-587-8570
301-587-8573 (fax)
www.ispi.org

ISBN 0-87425-924-X

Production services by Jean Miller
Editorial services by Sally Farnham
Cover design by Eileen Klockars

Table of Contents

Acknowledgments and Credits

Our thanks go to Robert W. Carkhuff, Publisher of Human Resource Development Press, for encouraging us to create this series. I want to thank many former students for helping me think and grow to bring my work to this stage, including Ryan Watkins, Doug Leigh, and Ingrid Guerra. I appreciate the work of Mariano Bernardez who has made the concepts and tools come alive in the operational world in this hemisphere and in Europe. Also, my thanks for the advice of the editors for this series, Dale Brethower and Richard Gerson, who have pushed (sometimes unsuccessfully) to make this work both useful and clear. They were joined by Ingrid Guerra in giving me specific, targeted, and often uncomfortable good advice.

Appreciation is extended to the Sonora Institute of Technology (ITSON) Mexico for providing a continuing laboratory for the concepts and tools in this book, both in planning and implementation based on adding societal value.

I also thank the many publishers who have brought earlier works that serve as important bases for this book to professional attention, including Sage/Corwin, Jossey-Bass/ Pfeiffer, Educational Technology, ISPI (including *Performance & Improvement* and *Performance Improvement Quarterly*), and several publications of the ASTD.

Finally, my thanks to the reader for choosing to examine, consider, and hopefully apply this work to help them define and achieve measurable success.

Roger Kaufman
April, 2006

Introduction

We are what we do—and accomplish.

Our choices and decisions about what we do and don't do determine the results we get. We are responsible for what we choose, and we can choose to be successful: to design and deliver results that provide measurable value.

The obvious theme here is choice: choices about what to plan and how best to deliver success. We can choose to be successful and get useful results, or we can choose to keep doing what we are now doing and harvesting what we now receive back for our efforts.

Doesn't it make sense to know where you are headed and that the intended destination is the right place to go? Mega thinking and planning is about defining and justifying where your organization heads before deciding on the best ways to improve performance. It pays to not let the "solutions cart" get in front of the "destination horse"—to select ends before means. This book is about being proactive: defining and justifying where one should head before deciding how to get there.

Choices, Decisions, and Consequences

Defining, justifying, designing, and delivering useful organizational results are possible. Doing so is straightforward and practical. It only requires us to choose those concepts and tools that will help us select appropriate actions that will deliver measurable success.

Delivering useful results and proving it depend on several areas of choice, including selecting a frame of mind that puts planning, assessment, analysis, design, development, implementation, and evaluation—and the feedback for continual improvement that provides—in proper context. What you use, do, produce, and deliver must all align to add value—measurable value to an organization's internal and external stakeholders. You can choose to add value to your external stakeholders or limit your choice to your job and your organization. But the former option is suggested: adding measurable value to all internal and external stakeholders.

Another choice is about the size—or unit of analysis—we select for our improvement efforts. Usually choice is about the job or what goes in a small group. Another choice is about the entire organization as the focus for performance improvement. And still another choice, what this book is about, is to see everything we use, do, produce, and deliver as nested in our shared society. Sooner or later, we have to be called to account for what we accomplish in terms of adding value both inside and outside the organization. Think big. It will pay us all handsome dividends.

The practical choice is that there must be a partnership that seeks success for all stakeholders, both within and outside of the organization, by design and by intention.

Another choice is that the definition of the results to be achieved must be measurable, and the ways and means we use to get results have to be based on solid research, not on any "flavor of the month" or a trendy idea.

And everything we use, do, produce, and deliver must be aligned with each other as they add up to value outside the organization, including external clients and society. We call such a mindset, or orientation, *Mega thinking,* and the planning that comes from this is termed *Mega planning.*

Mega planning is about setting the framework for performance improvement so that the related parts of the system may be properly designed, developed, and implemented. This approach is analogous to locating or designing a house before buying the furniture and selecting the décor. This approach defines and justifies the specifications for the entire organization (the "house") that will allow one to design what goes on within the organization. The emphasis here is on *what* the organization must deliver so that effective and efficient means may be considered and selected: *what* before *how.*

There are useful concepts, tools, and techniques for performance system design and development.[1] Each of the tools and techniques for performance improvement depends on the organization heading in a useful direction—a direction best determined and verified by strategic thinking and planning.

The Mega thinking and planning process and concepts provided in this book should not be confused with related detailed performance improvement tools and approaches. Mega thinking involves determining what the organization should deliver and then designing and developing the operational ways and means to deliver the required success. Mega thinking and planning also better ensure that what is developed inside the organization will add value outside of it—alignment.

Mega thinking and planning have a primary focus of adding measurable value for all stakeholders. It is realistic, practical, and ethical.

Three Fundamentals for Defining and Delivering Organizational Success

Defining and then achieving sustained organizational success is possible. It relies on three basic concepts:

1. **A societal (Mega) value-added "frame of mind" or paradigm:** Your perspective about your organization, people, and our world. It focuses on an agreed-upon approach to adding value to all stakeholders.

2. **A shared determination and agreement on where to head and why:** All people who can and might be impacted by the shared objectives must agree on purposes and results criteria.

3. **Pragmatic and basic tools for planning, design, development, implementation, and continual improvement:** Defining and determining the "hows" of achieving performance that are required for success.

This book provides the basic concepts for thinking and planning Mega in order to define and deliver value—measurable value—to internal and external partners. Choices should be based on rational data in order to deliver useful results.

This book covers several related topics that will provide the concepts and tools required for defining and justifying where you and your organization should head and how to tell when you have arrived.

Main topics to help guide your strategic thinking and planning choices[2] include:

- Defining who the clients are and who benefits

- Outlining the basic questions each organization must ask and answer

- Providing the basic concepts and tools for delivering performance improvement and proving the value they add

- Using both change management and change creation (or reactive as well as proactive thinking and doing)

- Assessing needs and placing the needs (not wants) in priority order

- Using performance data to continually plan to get from current results to desired ones, and then use the criteria and performance to continually improve—fixing what isn't working and continuing that which is working

This approach sets the stage for performance system design and development: First find direction and then develop the ways and means to get from here to there. The details for building on the Mega plan by designing, developing, implementing, and evaluating detailed performance systems are provided elsewhere, including Brethower (2006), Gerson (2006), Carleton (2006), Watkins (2006), and Guerra (2006).

Let's get going. As we move along, examples, self-assessments, and exercises are provided for use by you and your partners on your journey toward success.

Endnotes

1. Approaches, concepts, and tools such as:

Rummler, G. A. (2004). *Serious performance consulting: According to Rummler.* Silver Spring, MD: International Society for Performance Improvement and the American Society for Training and Development.

Brethower, D. M., & Dams, P. C., (January 1999). Systems thinking (and systems doing). *Performance Improvement, 38 (1),* 37–52.

Brethower, D. M. (2006). *Performance Analysis: Knowing what to do and how.* Amherst, MA: HRD Press.

Briggs, L. J. (Ed.) (1977). *Instructional design: Principles and applications.* Englewood Cliffs, NJ: Educational Technology Publications.

Briggs, L. J., & Wager, W. W. (1982). *Handbook of procedures for the design of instruction* (2nd ed.). Englewood Cliffs, NJ: Educational Technology Publications.

Dick, W., & Carey, L. (1989). *The systematic design of instruction* (3rd ed.). Glenview, IL: Scott Foresman & Co.

Gagne, R. M., & Driscoll, M. P. (1988). *Essentials of learning for instruction* (2nd ed.). NJ: Prentice-Hall.

Rothwell, W. J., & Kazanas, H. L. (1998). *Mastering the instructional design process: A systematic approach.* San Francisco, CA: Jossey-Bass Publishers.

Van Tiem, D. M., Moseley, J. L., & Dessinger, J. C. (2000). *Fundamentals of performance technology: A guide to improving people, process, and performance.* Silver Spring, MD: International Society for Performance Improvement.

Watkins, R. (2006). *Performance by design.* Amherst, MA: HRD Press.

2. This book and the guidance in it are linked with ten standards for performance improvement sponsored by ISPI. This is true of this book as well as the other five books in the series. The relationship to these published standards is found at the end of this book along with a suggestion on how existing standards could and should be expanded.

Chapter 1
Defining Where to Head and
Why to Go There

Could there be any more basic decision than where you and your organization should head, and justifying why you want to get there? It seems rational that the destination and what constitutes success for you and your organization would have to be agreed upon.

Yet organizations—public and private—have fuzzy statements of purpose.[1] You can, however, help modify this dismal and almost universal state of affairs and be much better off for your efforts. Everyone benefits from the positive changes you can make for precision, rigor, and delivered success.

Defining where we should head and justifying why we want to get there should be based on adding value to all stakeholders. Those stakeholders include external clients, our shared society, and our internal partners.

Deciding where to head is best nested in reality—the reality of economics, politics, and society. Change is ever present, and we can be the masters of change or the victims of it. Because there is change, we have choices, and those choices we make have consequences. We can choose success or choose something else.

The Three Cs of Life

There are three Cs of life:

- **C**hange
- **C**hoice
- **C**onsequences

We can count on change happening: We can take control or wait for things to happen to us. We may be proactive or reactive. This book starts at the proactive and sets the stage for reactive (and useful) performance system design and development.

We make choices in our personal lives as well as in our organization. We can choose to take control or be victims. Not making a decision is a decision.

And no matter what we do, or don't do, there are conse-quences—results or impacts. We are responsible for the conse-quences in our lives. We can improve our own odds by knowing about and controlling change through our choices—the three Cs of life.[2]

Change!

Change is scary for most of us. We know how to deal with today—whatever comes our way based on our current decisions and their consequences or payoffs. Some would rather deal with current reality than get out of their comfort zones and take a risk—a risk to change what we do and how we act. We can get beyond our history and our conventional ways of thinking and acting.

If we are not getting the payoffs—results—we want, then it seems only reasonable to change our behavior: to change what we do and how we do it. Simply said, we are what we do and accom-plish. If we want to get different results, then we must:

1. Define the results we are getting now.

2. Determine the results we want to get.

3. Establish what actions and behaviors will deliver the results we want to get us from current results and conse-quences to desired results and consequences.

4. Select new actions and behaviors.

5. Decide to change.

6. Change.

7. Support ourselves in our changed behaviors and actions and be prepared to change again if we don't get the results and payoffs we want.[3]

Here are some basic decision-making steps, based on Harold Greenwald's work:[4]

•   Identify the payoffs you are getting now that you don't want.

•   Identify the behaviors you are displaying that deliver the negative payoffs.[5]

- Identify the payoffs you do want.

- Identify the behaviors that will deliver the desired payoffs.

- Decide to change your behavior.

- Change.

- Be ready to decide to change in the future if you want different payoffs.

When we talk about decisions and changes, please think of these basic steps. This book provides the concepts and tools for defining and then making successful decisions.

Why change? What is really riskier? Continuing on with the predictable-yet-painful (or perhaps just boring and unrewarding) or deciding to make things better?

Choices

We do make choices. Not making choices is a choice. We can be the master of change or the victim of it, all depending on our choices. No matter our choices, the consequences are ours to own. We have to commit to our choices and carry them through until we get the results we desire.

Consequences

What happens to us in our lives is largely up to us. If bad things happen, we can be resilient or we can give up and drift from day to day. Means—our choices about change—lead to ends, results, and consequences. It seems smart to link our choices to the consequences we want and not leave it up to what fate and indecision deal us.

The basic choice for any planning is what frame of reference we will use:

- Will we choose to plan for our workgroup[6] as the primary beneficiary?

- Will we choose to plan for our organization as the primary beneficiary?

or

- Will we choose our external clients and society as the primary beneficiary of everything we use, do, produce, and deliver?

Successful strategic planning and strategic thinking—creating our future—are based on defining where to go and justifying why you want to get there. The basis for "where to go" and "why get there" resides in a simple but often overlooked reality: We all are means to societal ends. You, me, our organizations are all means to societal ends. When we think strategically, we focus on adding value to our shared society, and then we plan strategically to get measurable societal results.

Because of this fundamental reality (which is usually assumed or avoided) of basing everything we use, do, produce, and deliver on adding measurable value to external clients and society, this concept is provided now—front and center.

Society, Mega, and the Rational Choice

The basic rational choice is to make external clients and society—Mega—the planning frame. When you do, it is the safest, most practical, and ethical choice. When we choose our external clients and our shared society (Mega-level thinking and planning) as our planning frame, we can then sensibly align our workgroups and our organization to add value as we move from internal contributions to external ones.[7] This guiding principle is simple and straightforward, and it makes intuitive sense.

From this shared societal value-added frame,[8] everything you and your organization use, do, produce, and deliver is linked to achieve shared and agreed-upon positive societal results. Mega thinking (your mindset, or frame of reference based on adding value to our shared communities and society) is guided by an *Ideal Vision*,[9] which is defined in Figure 1.1. Note that the label *Ideal Vision* is just that, ideal. We might not get there in our lifetime or the lifetime of our children, but if that is not where we are headed, where do we stop? Consider this definition of an Ideal Vision that has been derived from asking people from around the world "What kind of world do you want to help create for tomorrow's child?"[10]

Why does using Mega make sense? It is rational if for no other reason than we all depend on each other for contributing to our safety, survival, and well-being. Thinking and planning Mega, however, is a choice, and like all other choices, you are responsible for the consequences of your choices.[11]

Here are some choices that you and your organization face:

- Add value to our organization while adding value to our shared world (Mega) **or** only add value to myself and my organization

- Enlarge the frame of reference for planning and doing **or** keep the current focus on the organization alone or small groups within the organization

- Focus on immediate effectiveness (results and consequences) now and in the future **or** focus on efficiency (the ease of doing things)

Choices: If you don't choose Mega, what do you choose? What results and consequences will you take responsibility for delivering and not delivering?

Figure 1.1: An Ideal Vision.

Basic Ideal Vision: The world we want to help create for tomorrow's child
There will be no loss of life nor elimination or reduction of levels of survival, self-sufficiency, or quality of life from any source including (but not limited to) the following: - War, riot, terrorism, or unlawful civil unrest - Unintended human-caused changes to the environment including permanent destruction of the environment and/or rendering it non-renewable - Murder, rape, or crimes of violence, robbery, or destruction to property - Substance abuse - Shelter

(Continued)

Figure 1.1 (Concluded)

- Permanent or continuing disabilities
- Disease
- Starvation and/or malnutrition
- Destructive behavior (including child, partner, spouse, self, elder, others)
- Accidents, including transportation, home, and business/workplace
- Discrimination based on irrelevant variables including color, race, age, creed, gender, religion, wealth, national origin, or location

Consequences: Poverty will not exist, and every woman and man will earn at least as much as it costs them to live unless they are progressing toward being self-sufficient and self-reliant. No adult will be under the care, custody, or control of another person, agency, or substance. All adult citizens will be self-sufficient and self-reliant as minimally indicated by their consumption being equal to or less than their production.

The choice might not be comfortable at first, but if you are not adding value to our shared society, what assurance do you have that you are not subtracting value?[12] Starting with Mega as the central focus, *strategic thinking* provides the database—foundation—for *strategic planning.*

Note: This will not be the last time Mega is presented or discussed. More detail and applications are in the following chapters and it is the central theme of this book: proactive action to define what must be accomplished to improve our shared world before fixing and repairing what we are now using and doing.

A central question that each and every organization should ask and answer is:

If your organization is the solution, what's the problem?

This fundamental proposition is central to thinking and planning strategically—using a Mega focus. It represents a shift from focusing on oneself, individual performance improvement, and one's organization to making certain you also add value to external clients and society. In working with your organization, ask the above question. The dialog that will result usually lets people know that they and the organization are only a means to societal ends. If the organization is not adding measurable value to external clients and society, its time is short. Many organizations, such as the ill-fated "dot.coms," and too many high-rolling companies, including those that have gone bankrupt and/or whose executives are serving jail time, failed to ask this question.

Instead of asking this question, most organizations typically stop at what is immediately good for them and their organization (the so-called bottom line or business case) and neglect to make sure they and their organization are adding value outside of themselves. Some organizations pull up the cloak of Corporate Social Responsibility (CSR) and dodge their responsibility to add value directly to our shared society by building swings for playgrounds, sponsoring "5% days" where that percentage of all sales goes to charity, or working in the community.

Such "feel good" responses to social responsibility might look good, but it still must be augmented by (and perhaps be secondary to) each organization and each person in the organization making sure that everything they use, do, produce, and deliver adds direct value to their external clients and our shared world. For example, United Parcel Service (UPS) does both community as well as charity outreach. In the performance of their organization worldwide, they set objectives and use hard performance indicators to track environmental and safety contributions.[13]

A dual center of attention on and direct contribution to our shared society seems to be growing as it should be. Making money and doing societal good must not be mutually exclusive.

The use of the label *Corporate Social Responsibility (CSR)* might signal a growing interest in societal consequences. Even the worldwide managing director of McKinsey & Company, Ian Davis, has noted that the early and narrowly applied Milton Friedman admonition of "the business of business is business" has outlived its usefulness.[14] This is especially true if it means looking at last quarter's financial results as the only measure of success. Just looking after the bottom line is no longer enough. Viable CSR should include rigorous indicators of measurable societal value added to its scorecard, not just tinkering with some of the possible elements of adding social value.

Sensibly and happily, organizations are joining the chorus that adding societal value is not only necessary ethically, but also makes good business sense.[15] Increasing examples of measurable results from thinking and acting Mega are now finding their way into publication.[16] This represents a shift away from the usual and aging concept that the business's sole focus on the bottom line may be giving way to an additional and primary focus on Mega thinking and planning.[17] Adding societal value and using both your talents and your organization's talents are practical, smart, and safe.

The hallmark of this approach to strategic planning and think-ing—Mega thinking and planning—suggested in this book is a focus on society and using yourself and your organization as the vehicle for adding value. In considering this, here are two questions:

- What are the risks for not thinking, planning, and doing Mega?

- What are the risks for thinking, planning, and doing Mega?

Indicator for Mega Results for Individuals: Measuring Results and Consequences

Measurement is both vital and tricky. How do we know when some-one is self-sufficient and self-reliant? When can we tell when they are not under the care, custody, or control of another person or agency? Good questions, and ones for which we should have answers.

In the Ideal Vision (Figure 1.1), we note that each individual should at least be self-sufficient and self-reliant. But how can we tell? One useful indicator[18] is that a person's consumption (what he or she pays for) is equal to or less than his or her production (what he or she gets paid for). A simple equation is:

$$C \leq P$$

where C is consumption (in monies paid out) and P is production (for which one gets income). This is an indicator of self-sufficiency and self-reliance.

Additional indicators might be used for individuals:

- Making more than you spend
- Not in jail
- Not on government transfer payments (e.g., welfare, relief, food stamps, charity, etc.)
- Positive credit rating
- Not in an institution for the mentally impaired
- Not homeless
- Not in any situation where you're dependent on the kindness of others or government support

Is this all a bit mercenary? Perhaps. It is also practical and pragmatic.

No matter the culture, there is always some token of exchange, be it pounds, yen, dollars, euros, shells, or cattle. We keep track in terms of some form of money. Does such an indicator cover all possible criteria or does this give a perfect fit with actual survival, self-sufficiency, and quality of life? No, but at least it provides some metrics for us to use and improve.

What If My Boss or My Associates Are Not Ready for Mega?

They might not be at first. You may have to help them see the wisdom in their making better choices. And recent concerns in mainstream business as well as public sector organizations (both in the United States and abroad) show that a primary focus on societal value added is evolving.

But you can educate others, including your boss. You can help them see the benefits of thinking and planning Mega as compared to the costs for not doing so. If they don't want to add value to their clients and the shared communities and society in which we all live, what do they have in mind? Who will be called to account for not adding measurable value to all stakeholders? Will they be able to defend their decisions in the harsh light of publicity?

When there is initial resistance, it is often about fear: fear of not knowing how to add societal value, fear that no one else is now doing that, or fear that they don't have enough control over what gets used, done, produced, and delivered in terms of the impact all of that has on both the bottom line and consequences for our world.[19]

One possibility for not seeing the importance of Mega focus is saliency—how important it is to a person. If a person doesn't see survival and self-sufficiency staring them in the eye—no immediacy—they might defer doing anything about Mega. The closer one is to the survival level (such as in a war, facing a devastating health situation, impending natural disaster, imminent threat, etc.), the more Mega seems important. To deal with possible denial is to help people see the real links between what they use, do, produce, and deliver and measurable societal consequences. When given the cool and rational opportunity to consider their choices—organizational alone or organizational plus external clients and society—most make the practical choice. To help, a decision guide is presented in Figure 1.2 for working with others to get agreement on Mega.

A Basis for Dialog with Others About Thinking and Planning Mega

With current planning partners (including your bosses), start this dialog with their responses as well as yours. The gaps that you get for each and all questions will let everyone know what is involved in thinking and planning with a Mega frame. It will also allow them to consider the implications of *not* doing the actions in statements #1 through #4 in Figure 1.2.

The assessment in Figure 1.2 can serve as an agreement process to get all in your organization as well as your external partners going to the same destination—to align with them. Have all your partners and stakeholders fill this form out, and compare the gaps between What Is and What Should Be for each statement. When there is disagreement about the gaps, begin a dialog. Ask why you differ, and what are the implications of not consistently doing each and all of the four items.

Figure 1.2: A basis for a dialog about commitment to adding value to all internal and external stakeholders

Rarely, if ever	Almost Never	Not Usually	Quite Frequently	Consistently	← WHAT IS / WHAT SHOULD BE →	Rarely, if ever	Almost Never	Not Usually	Quite Frequently	Consistently
					Indicate the relative frequency with which the following statements are true concerning the "drivers" for the way you make decisions. Please provide two responses to each question.					
					Describe how you see yourself currently operating. / **Describe how you think you should be operating.**					
					1. The total organization will contribute to clients' and societal survival, health, and well-being.					
					2. The total organization will contribute to clients' and societal quality of life.					
					3. Clients' and societal survival, health, and well-being will be the focus of the organization's and each of its facility's mission objectives.					
					4. Each organizational operational function will have objectives that contribute to #1, #2, and #3 above.					

Ask yourself, and the others with whom you are partners, "If we are not doing these, what do we have in mind?" Such an exercise will let people step back from their everyday existence and pressures and consider other choices. And consider other consequences that flow from their current decisions and consequences. When anyone decides to not apply Mega, remember that they are responsible for the consequences of their choice.

Mega thinking and planning is the responsible and responsive choice. An increasing number of organizations are now using Mega as their frame of reference, and still others are moving toward it.[20]

Mega thinking and planning are what this book is about. Based on that, let's get into the concepts and then to the tools for adding measurable value.

Endnotes

1. Kaufman, R., Watkins, R., Triner, D., & Stith, M. (1998).

2. Richard Gerson suggests a fourth C: Commitment.

3. This approach is based on my work in needs assessment and planning and the psychotherapy model developed by the late Harold Greenwald's *Direct Decision Therapy* (Greenwald, H. (1973). Decision *therapy.* NY: Peter Wyden, Inc.). It is further expanded in my *30 Seconds That Can Change Your Life,* also published by HRD Press (2006).

4. These are the basic steps of Greenwald's *Direct Decision Therapy.* They are powerful and rational and are practical for everyday life.

5. Payoffs are the rewards and consequences of our decisions.

6. This book has a primary focus on organizations, both public and private. However, please keep in mind that the concepts and tools provided here can be applied to personal and family life.

7. Figure 3.1 in Chapter 3 shows the three levels of planning and results.

8. The process for defining and using Mega relies on the democratic process of all people who could be impacted by the definition of Mega coming to agreement.

9. This was derived by asking, informally, people from around the globe (not formally including Central Africa or the former Soviet Union, however) to define the world they would create for their children and grandchildren. In earlier work (Kaufman, Oakley-Browne, Watkins, & Leigh, 2003), this was also called "mother's rule" because when mothers, regardless of culture, are asked the kind of world they want for their children, they don't talk to means and resources but rather to ends and consequences related to self-sufficiency and self-reliance.

10. Based on Kaufman (1998, 2000); Kaufman, Oakley-Browne, Watkins, & Leigh (2003); Kaufman, Guerra, & Platt (2006).

11. In earlier work, I called the use of Mega "practical dreaming"—a concept that management expert Wess Roberts thought appropriate enough to reference in his writings.

12. Not all people see merit (and some even see danger) in using a Mega focus (Schneider [2003]; Winiecki [2004]). Along with others, including Brethower (2005), I find such objections to be either wrong or naïve.

13. See the United Parcel Service's "sustainability report" at http://www.sustainability.ups.com/popup/performance/main.html.

14. Ian Davis (2005) noted some of the following as sensible corporate behavior relative to strategic planning and corporate responsibility:

    - Organizations must shift away from the "create shareholder value" model to social contribution.

    - Organizations must build social issues into strategy.

    - "Social issues are not so much tangential to the business of business as fundamental to it."

    - Companies that treat social issues as either irritating distractions or simply unjustified vehicles for attacks on business are turning a blind eye to impending forces that have the potential to alter the strategic future in fundamental ways.

    - The "business of business is business" outlook obscures the requirement to address questions about their ethics and legitimacy.

    - There is an implicit contract between big business and society.

    - Business leaders have to shape the debate on social issues by establishing ever higher (but appropriate) standards of integrity and transparency.

    - Rousseau's social contract helped to seed the idea that leaders must serve the public good, lest their own legitimacy be threatened. Today's CEOs should take the opportunity to restate and reinforce their own social contracts in order to help secure, for the long term, the invested billions of their shareholders.

        The Economist. London: May 26, 2005. From Ian Davis, worldwide managing director of McKinsey & Company.

15. Davis, I. (2005, May 26). The biggest contract. *The Economist,* 375 (8428), 87. London: May 28, 2005.

16. For example, a special issue on Mega: *Performance Improvement Quarterly*, Volume 18, Number 3. In this issue are case studies of the applications of Mega thinking and planning in the private and public sectors in cultures ranging from the United States to Australia to Argentina to the United Kingdom to Africa. Articles include:

Bernardez, M. (2005). Achieving business success by developing clients and community: Lessons from leading companies, emerging economies and a nine year case study. *Performance Improvement Quarterly, 18*(3), 37–55.

Clark, S. E., & Murray, M. (2005). Mega-planning in population. *Performance Improvement Quarterly, 18*(3), 17–25.

Forbes, R., Forbes, D., & Haskins, P. (2005). Start-up Mega—A case history. *Performance Improvement Quarterly, 18*(3), 100–110.

Garratt, B. (2005). Can boards of directors think strategically? Some issues in developing direction-givers' thinking to a Mega level. *Performance Improvement Quarterly, 18*(3), 26–36.

Guerra, I. Outcome-based vocational rehabilitation: Measuring valuable results. *Performance Improvement Quarterly, 18*(3), 65–75.

Guerra, I., Bernardez, M., Jones, M., & Zidan, S. (2005). Government workers adding value: The Ohio workforce development program. *Performance Improvement Quarterly, 18*(3), 76–99.

Guerra, I., & Rodriguez, G. (2005). Educational planning and social responsibility: Eleven years of Mega planning at the Sonora Institute of Technology (ITSON). *Performance Improvement Quarterly, 18*(3), 56–64.

Kaufman, R. (2005). Defining and delivering measurable value: A Mega thinking and planning primer. *Performance Improvement Quarterly, 18*(3), 8–16.

Kaufman, R., & Bernardez, M. (Eds.) (2005). *Performance Improvement Quarterly, 18*(3), 3–5.

Uranga, S., & Lucellas, M. C. (2005). Using Mega planning in CSO projects—Bringing social sectors together for measurable and sustainable social impact. *Performance Improvement Quarterly, 18*(3), 111–116.

17. I am getting less lonely since my first publication on the importance of all organizations adding measurable value to our shared society in 1969. (Kaufman, R. A., Corrigan, R. E., & Johnson, D. W. (1969). Towards educational responsiveness to society's needs: A tentative utility model. *Journal of Socio-Economic Planning Sciences, 3,* 151–157.) Joining the call for a focus on societal contribution was futurist Faith Popcorn (Popcorn, F. [1991]. *The Popcorn Report.* New York: Doubleday) who noted that doing societal good is no longer a corporate option, but a must.

    Still, there are those who believe that the starting and end-point of any performance improvement effort is the "business case." This is limiting because that business-case focus almost never formally looks at a proactive approach to adding societal value. The world is catching up concerning Mega and adding value to our shared society, as well it must. With a little bit of luck, Mega thinking, planning, and doing might be close to the "tipping point."

18. Based on our research and program experiences.

19. Jan Kaufman provided this insight.

20. A special issue of *Performance Improvement Quarterly* (2005) has eight articles concerning applications of Mega thinking and planning. Still more attention to this is provided in Kaufman (1998, 2000), Kaufman, Oakley-Browne, Watkins, & Leigh (2003), as well as Kaufman, Watkins, Triner, & Stith (1998) among others.

Chapter 2
New Times, New Concepts, New Realities: Choosing Success

Mega thinking and planning is a matter of choice. You can select success and do what is required to create it, or you may choose to stay comfortable in how you think about problems and opportunities—comfortable for the moment until you are overtaken by reality. Any decision to change or keep going is in a context of new realities that exist.

New Realities for Organizational Success

To be successful—to do and apply Mega thinking and planning—you have to realize that yesterday's concepts, biases, understandings, stereotypes, and methods and their associated results are often not always appropriate for tomorrow. Most planning experts agree that the past is only prologue, and tomorrow must be crafted through new patterns of perspectives, tools, and results.[1] Figure 2.1 presents basic new realities that "drive" our world.

Figure 2.1: Basic new realities that "drive" our world.
(based, in part, on Kaufman [1998, 2000]).

Basic New Realities
• Tomorrow is not a linear projection of yesterday: You can't solve today's problems with the same paradigms and tools that created them.
• If we cannot predict the future, create it. (Peter Drucker)
• After September 11, 2001 (and then Bali, Madrid, London, and natural disasters[2]), we know we can no longer *just* focus on individual performance improvement—"system<u>s</u> approaches."

(Continued)

Figure 2.1 (Concluded)

- Reality is not divided into jobs, functions, departments, organizations, issues, or laws.

- Everything we use, do, produce, and deliver must add value at the societal level—a "system approach."[3]

- Don't be the best of the best...be the only one who does what you do. (Jerry Garcia)

- Operate as if you intend to put your organization out of business through success.

- Compliance is nowhere near as important as competence.

- Useful change has to add value for all internal and external partners.

- Fix the problem, not the blame.

- There are two bottom lines for any organization: conventional and societal.

What does each of these new realities mean? And why are they important when we move to authentic strategic thinking and planning? We will answer these questions for each new reality below.

New Reality: *Tomorrow is not a linear projection of yesterday: You can't solve today's problems with the same paradigms and tools that created them.*

If we stay locked into the idea that change is gradual or incremental, and all we have to do is become more efficient at what we already do, we are likely to choose a disaster plan. Who would want to use the business ethics of yesterday—of Tyco, WorldCom, Enron, Andersen?

Who would want to keep using the tools and techniques of accounting, planning, and development that created the disaster plans of the past? One old idea has been "If it ain't broke, don't fix it." But if we do not continually improve, we will leave things alone as they become obsolete, and even dangerous. Another idea has been "You can't do business with people who don't have money, but new thinking and new paradigms have shown that you can; by showing people how to make and save money."[4]

Things change very rapidly and sometimes thrust the demand for change upon us; we must be reactive, quick, and right. We also should be proactive and create the kind of world we want for tomorrow's child—Mega results and payoffs. Creating this kind of world, using our organizations and our jobs as the vehicle for doing that, leads us to another new reality.

New Reality: *If we cannot predict the future, create it.*

Creating the future we want for our children and grandchildren will allow us to create change, not be overtaken by it. While we must respond to unpredicted change, we may choose to create our world of tomorrow, or organization of tomorrow, and our jobs of tomorrow.

This advice provided by Professor Peter Drucker—arguably the most insightful, knowledgeable, and brilliant of modern-day management experts—is indeed profound. Most efforts for change are reactive; they try to react to waves of change as they wash over us, or fret about trends that are predicted based on current and conventional wisdom. The truth is closer to the fact that we can look out for what might be coming our way, but our crystal ball gets very murky further out than tomorrow. So simply wait for change to respond? The late great Peter Drucker urges not. We should identify the world we want to create and go about doing just that. It is elegant, brilliant, and simple.

In fact, this new reality is a basic driver for Mega thinking and Mega planning: We can be the victims of change or the masters of it. Why not use ourselves and our organizations as the vehicle for creating our future? Why not indeed? And Mega thinking and planning will allow us to do that—to move ever closer to the world we would create for tomorrow's child.

New Reality: *After September 11, 2001 (and then Bali, Madrid, London, and natural disasters[5]), we know we can no longer just focus on individual performance improvement—"systems approaches."*

In our field, we often use words in a slippery manner. Terms that frequently get mixed up together are *system approach, systems approach, systematic approach,* and *systemic approach.* We use them as if they were the same.

Not to be pedantic or stuffy, these words and concepts are not the same—not by a long shot. These differences are really important, and it might have taken our perceptions and assumptions before September 11, 2001, to re-examine what we use, do, produce, and deliver and to make some subtle but important distinctions among some words: *system approach, systems approach, systematic approach,* and *systemic approach.*[6] These words show a difference in the unit of analysis we focus on.

> ***System Approach:*** An inclusive focus that begins with the sum total of parts working independently and together to achieve a useful set of results at the societal level...adding value for all internal and external partners. We best think of it as the large whole as illustrated below:

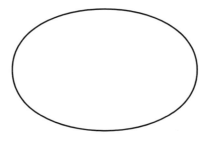

A system is composed of smaller subsystems (see "systems approach" below) that form a larger system. Each of these parts works independently and together.

Usually, people who ignore the external client/societal focus of an organization start their planning and doing with one or more of the subsystems, but call each a "system." Thus the confusion arises between a *system* approach that is holistic and starts with a focus on Mega, and a *systems* approach that looks only at one or more of the *parts* of the overall system. This is important (and not semantic quibbling because only dealing with the subsystems and not the whole system will deliver failure down the road). It would be like getting into physical shape by exercising your abs, but not realizing that there are many more body subsystems that make up your overall health, vigor, and well-being.

Systems Approach: A narrow focus that begins with the parts of a system—or the subsystems—that make up the "system," as illustrated below:

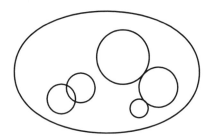

It should be noted that the "system" as portrayed here is made up of smaller elements, or subsystems (shown as bubbles), imbedded in the larger system. If we start at this smaller level, we will start with a part and not the whole. So, when someone says they are using a systems approach, they are really focusing on one or more subsystems; they are unfortunately focusing on the parts—splinters—and not the whole. When planning and doing at this level, they can only *assume* that the payoffs and consequences will add up to something useful to society and external clients.

It is possible that many governmental and political problems come from each agency, entity, or organization looking at themselves as "the system" and limiting themselves to their own good and not also looking at the larger system in which we all live, work, and contribute. For example, each state and federal agency generally submits budgets for themselves without any formal criteria for measuring the extent to which they add value to our shared society. Thus, each agency (e.g., FBI, Homeland Security, Defense, Health and Human Services) struggles to capture a significant part of a limited overall federal budget; they are competitive with each other instead of cooperative for the common societal good.[7]

When organizations compete with each other, the opportunities for cooperation and synergies tend to remain unexamined or ignored. The way in which we conventionally plan and budget, based on splinters of the whole (my organization, my group, my service) and not the whole (Mega), might be contributing to poor results.

Systematic Approach: An approach that does things in an orderly, predictable, and controlled manner. It is a reproducible process. Doing things, however, in a systematic manner does not ensure the achievement of useful results. Some major atrocities that civilization has experienced have been quite systematic.

Systemic Approach: An approach that affects everything in the system. The definition of "the system" is usually left up to the practitioner and thus may or may not include external clients and society; it might not (and usually does not in practice) include Mega. It does not necessarily mean that when something is systemic it is also useful.

So what do these distinctions have to do with September 11, 2001, terrorism, and any new reality? Plenty. There is a lesson to be learned here that can be generalized to everything we do. Let's see:

During the security programs prior to this horrific attack, the concern was driven by airlines that pushed for "depart on time" and the screener's job was to focus on each passenger being screened and getting quickly to the boarding gate and not upon a system driver of "arrive alive." Thus, by policy on that fateful day, it was legal to bring a box cutter on board.

But because the focus was on system<u>s</u> (each passenger and meeting existing screening requirements) and not on the system—arrive alive—screeners did not perceive a potential problem coming from the fact that five independent people boarding a flight all had box cutters. The unit of analysis we use in performance improvement and accomplishment shapes that we use, do, produce, and develop, and a systems (actually a subsystems) frame of reference will make us miss the required alignment between all the levels of the Organizational Elements Model—Guide 1, Figure 3.1—and oversimplify our view and thus limit our results.

It is vital that we link everything we use, do, produce, and deliver to adding measurable value to ourselves, our organizations, and our external clients and shared society: a *system approach.* This gives rise to another new reality.

New Reality: *Reality is not divided into jobs, functions, departments, organizations, issues, or laws.*

Look at any organization chart, and you immediately realize that is not the way the organization really works. All of those cascades of names in boxes with titles in each are a convenient function. Organizations don't work that way.

Consider the way politicians talk about "issues." Each issue is a splinter of the whole social landscape, and if we look at each one at a time—a systems approach—we miss the whole. But they pass single-issue laws and wonder why the legislation doesn't deliver desired results. They look at health delivery without linkages to transportation (to get services) or economics. We pass educational testing legislation without looking to see if passing the tests relates to success in life. These are all splinters, parts, and hunks that are not related to the whole.

Yet the conventional wisdom and conventional approaches to performance improvement are single-issue-focused. We attack specific jobs to improve each without really seeing if that job adds value to all other related jobs and to what the organization delivers externally.[8]

The organizational elements—what an organization uses, does, produces, delivers, and the external contributions—help to avoid splintering and fragmentation. For any improvement initiative, look at both the whole as well as the parts. Ensure that each of the organizational elements (defined in full in Chapter 3, Figure 3.1 and Chapter 4, Figure 4.2) are done rigorously and correctly and ensure that they are all aligned one with the others so that what any organization uses, does, produces, and delivers outside of itself adds value to our shared world:

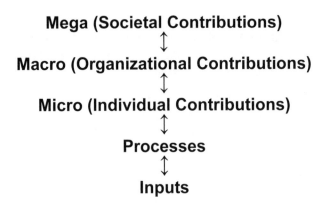

Ensuring the alignment will deliver results that add up—that will add value to all internal and external stakeholders. Simply focusing on one or two of the elements will likely result in our failure. After all, we live in a world where we and our organizations are nothing more (or nothing less) than means to societal ends.

System, Systems, Systematic, and Systemic

The Organizational Elements Model describes a total system—a system made up of many parts. It has its primary focus on adding value to external clients and society: on Mega. What gets delivered outside the organization, Marco, is made up of all the building-block results accomplished at the Micro level. And Micro-level results, in turn, come from processes, means, and activities using human, capital, and physical resources: inputs. An operational system, such as your organization, contains and uses all of the organizational elements. The Organizational Elements Model describes the relationships of any system. The application and use of the Organizational Elements Model is dynamic and interactive. The relationship among the organizational elements is not linear. This alignment lets you know that everything that is done and accomplished at the Micro, Macro, and Mega levels is built on processes and inputs. In a dynamic system—and that is every organization—there is a constant back-and-forth flow among all of the elements.

For example, performance system design and development (C.F. Rummler [2004] and Brethower [2006]) is a process that systematically finds what is required for successful performance and provides it to people in the organization. The organization that chooses to improve its performance becomes the system, and design, development, implementation, and continual improvement are built upon inputs and other processes. This organization delivers—at the Micro, then Macro, then Mega levels—measurable value. Based on design and development, gaining information from each of the organizational elements allows for the organization and the people in it to change what should be changed and continue that which is working. Any changes to the system being improved are intended to be systematic; the processes and methods are known and transparent. And impacting everything used, done, and delivered will add value to the entire system: be systemic.

To better ensure that splintering doesn't take place, the organizational elements provide a guide for making sure everything is in place and aligned. The actual change is focused on the target system: the organization to be improved.]

Is All of This Making Too Much of a Big Deal about Words and Definitions?

It might seem so at first, but the answer is "no." Precision and rigor are keys to defining, achieving, and proving success. Our work is too important to let our efforts deteriorate into an *Alice in Wonderland* world of "Words mean anything I want them to mean: nothing more and nothing less." Words stand for realities, and we want to make sure that we agree on what we are talking about. Because we make decisions that impact us as well as others, we must care deeply that we are headed in the right direction, and that we are very rigorous and precise in choosing our methods and criteria for evaluating our success.

Some choose to use words that are comfortable to others rather than take the risk of asking people to change their ways. What usually happens is that people get stuck in their existing paradigms and never shift.[9]

(In a spirit of responsiveness, as we go, we define words and concepts as well as provide a Glossary at the end of the book. A few more times we will give what might seem to be unique definitions for words. These definitions and their use will be very valuable for you, even though they may differ from the common definitions of the terms. It will be worth your while to consider these unique definitions.)

New Reality: *Everything we use, do, produce, and deliver must add value at the societal level—a "system approach."*

This is not conventional wisdom. The old paradigms were "The business of business is business," "What's good for our company is good for the world," "The bottom line is our most important concern," "We look after the business, and the government looks after the people." These paradigms are completely self-absorbed and totally out of touch with reality.

It is vital to our success that we look beyond the conventional boundaries of planning and doing—look beyond the business case, the quarterly profits, or any one organization, division, department, or group. Our success hinges on our relating and relying everything we use, do, produce, and deliver on adding value to our shared society—our world and our universe. If we don't, we develop only a part of the whole and not the entire whole.

When making decisions, ask "Will this add value to all internal and external stakeholders?" If not, revisit your decision criteria. Making money and doing societal good should not and must not be mutually exclusive.

We expect everyone we deal with to put our health and safety as the number one thing on their priority list. And we should do the same for them. Think for a moment about the organizations that you do business with regularly, both in work and in life. Using the chart in Figure 2.2 on the following page, indicate which organizations you are willing to have put their profits above your survival, health, and well-being?

It is difficult to find any organization with which we deal that we, in some way, don't demand that they put us ahead of them. And the same goes for your job and your organization: others depend upon you putting them #1 on your priority list. Doing so is both practical and ethical.

If you don't add value to our shared world and our clients, you might be subtracting value.[10] You only have to look at the wreckage of selfish organizations worldwide in the late 1990s and early 2000s to see that greed is no longer in style, let alone legal.

Figure 2.2: Profits vs. health and safety.

Organization you do business with regularly	Check those where it is okay with you if they put profits ahead of your health, safety, and well-being
Airline	
Restaurant	
Grocery store	
Physician	
Dentist	
Insurance company	
Amusement park	
Automobile mechanic	
Tire manufacturer	
Other:	

Most people are a bit surprised, at first, to find that they already contribute to Mega—much more than they initially thought. The exercise in Figure 2.3 may be done by you and your organization to see if you are contributing and to see if there are other areas you might also add measurable value to our shared society by identifying your organization's *current* contributions to society.

Figure 2.3: Organization's current societal contributions.

Without formally recognizing the fact, all organizations impact external clients and society. For each of the basic components of an **Ideal Vision** (listed below), check if your organization currently makes a contribution to that element and thus to the total Ideal Vision—to Mega.[11]

Basic Ideal Vision Elements: *There will be no losses of life nor elimination or reduction of levels of well-being, survival, self-sufficiency, and quality of life from any source, including (but not limited to):*	Makes a Contribution		
	Directly	Indirectly	None
War, riot, terrorism, or unlawful civil unrest			
Unintended human-caused changes to the environment including permanent destruction of the environment and/or rendering it non-renewable			
Murder, rape, or crimes of violence, robbery, or destruction to property			
Substance abuse			
Shelter			
Disease			
Starvation and/or malnutrition			
Destructive behavior (abuse) including child, partner, spouse, self, elder, and others			
Accidents, including transportation, home, and business/workplace			
Discrimination based on irrelevant variables, including color, race, creed, sex, religion, national origin, age, location			

As a consequence of applying Mega thinking and planning, the following provides criteria for moving toward the Ideal Vision— moving toward Mega:

- Poverty will not exist, and every woman and man will earn at least as much as it costs them to live unless they are progressing toward being self-sufficient and self-reliant.

- No adult will be under the care, custody, or control of another person, agency, or substance: All adult citizens will be self-sufficient and self-reliant as minimally indicated by their consumption being equal to or less than their production.

- Any and all organizations—public and private—will contribute to the achievement and maintenance of this basic Ideal Vision and will be funded and continued to the extent to which it meets its objectives and the basic Ideal Vision is accomplished and maintained. People will be responsible for what they use, do, and contribute and thus will not contribute to the reduction of any of the results identified in this basic Ideal Vision.

> **Note:** Remember that an Ideal Vision is just that: ideal. It is the destination we choose to move relentlessly toward, calibrate our progress, and revise as required as we move from where we are to there.

What Usually Comes from Using This Exercise?

It is interesting that most people who go through this exercise realize that directly or indirectly they currently make at least some contribution to Mega—to our shared society. If there are policies about protecting their workers from external demonstrations, they are contributing to the first element of Mega. Choosing to add measurable value to our external clients and our shared society makes sense.

What about "being competitive?" Is that enough? If you are being competitive, you are always attempting to catch up with others. If you are the leader, they are always trying to catch up with you. Thus, there is another new reality:

New Reality: *Don't be the best of the best… be the only one who does what you do.* (Jerry Garcia of the Grateful Dead).

While you are ensuring your future and the future of your clients', it seems silly to benchmark others—to copy what they are doing. Silly? Indeed. Most people benchmark others (some call it "best practice") to copy a method, tool, or process without ever verifying that the objectives of that organization are a perfect match with their objectives. A process is only as useful as the results it delivers, so be sure that what you are importing will really contribute to your objectives.

And this goes hand in hand with the related concept of *strive for perfection.* Instead of benchmarking others, you should benchmark perfection.[12] Perfection? Yes. Everyone knows what perfection is—no rejects, no breakdowns, no accidents, no deaths, no disabilities, no losses. So why not see how close you and your organization can come to perfection? A Japanese car company, world-renown for quality, advertises their brand and relates that they are "in passionate pursuit of perfection." If you do pursue perfection, even though you might not get there right away, you will do what Jerry Garcia suggested: you won't be the best of the best, you will be the only one who does what you do—unique and successful.[13] And you add value to all stakeholders.

If you are unique and successful, others might want to knock you out of contention—to take away your business and success. Thus another new reality:

New Reality: *Operate as if you intend to put your organization out of business through success.*

If you do this, others will not easily catch up with you let alone overtake you. If someone intends to put you out of business, why don't you take the same approach? Constantly look to see what could put you out of business—perhaps a better, safer, less costly product, or something different that would replace your product—and be the one to create it. Stay fresh, stay open and creative, stay ahead.

One enemy of success is "good enough." It is tempting to rest on your laurels (as some giant U.S. manufacturers seem to be willing to do) and just improve the processes (continuous process improvement without results improvement) and be in compliance with existing standards. Thus another new reality is worth considering:

New Reality: *Compliance is nowhere near as important as competence.*

There is a cult of efficiency out there: continuous process improvement, efficiency, reducing variability,[14] meeting government regulations, etc. Is that good enough? Why would you want to improve the efficiency of any operation? Why would you simply strive to be compliant when you are not assured that what you are doing and delivering is useful?

You can be compliant and not be competent. You can use the accepted process, but still get ineffective or even harmful results. Competence is about getting the right job done at the right time with the required quality. Compliance is about following a process correctly. They are certainly not the same. As we noted earlier, effectiveness (getting useful results) is more important (if we can't have both) than efficiency (ease and simplicity of the process). Move first to define useful ends, then choose the means and resources. Simply doing what you are told—simply being compliant—might not deliver useful results for you, your group, or your organization.

While we are being competent, it is vital that whatever we use, do, produce, and deliver us useful to all of our partners, internal and external.

New Reality: *Useful change has to add value for all internal and external partners.*

Why? Greed and selfishness don't wear well, and they don't work well. The current government and business landscapes are littered with the consequences of looking after one's self instead of looking after everyone. People might be naïve, but they are not, at the end of the day, stupid. They can sense when one is pushing their own agenda and only giving lip service to helping you. Honesty and Mega go together.

Why would you want to cheat others with whom you work and upon which your future depends? What short-sighted thinking can lead one to talk about shared good, but to act selfishly? The old advice to treat others as you want to be treated is good. Adding value to all is ethical, sensible, and practical.

Instead of adding value to all stakeholders, sometimes people want to blame someone else for what happened (or didn't happen) and end up diverting their energies from learning from the experience—continual improvement—to attacking and criticizing. From this is another new reality:

New Reality: *Fix the problem, not the blame.*[15]

Fixing the blame seems to have become a blood sport in politics: blame, blame, blame. This ignores the fact that, from the language of Quality Management and Continual Improvement, every breakdown is a friend in disguise; you can use the failure to know what to change. Blaming is not useful in life, in evaluation, or in organizational behavior. Learn from what happened and use that to fix, not to blame.

And speaking of adding value for all, another new reality is:

New Reality: *There are two bottom lines for any organization: conventional and societal.*

It is the conventional (and old) wisdom that "the business of business is business" and that "business" is limited to short-term financial results. We see this limited view of business—one that focuses only on short-term gain—expressed often by most who talk about "business needs," "the business case," and "bottom-line thinking." Making a profit (if you are in the private sector) or getting desired funding (if you are in the public sector) is important. Of course, making money and profit is good, and doing so is required to stay in business and repay stockholders.

What if one just focuses on the conventional bottom line and ignores (or abuses) the societal bottom line—ignores adding measurable value for internal and external stakeholders? How long can an organization draw down from our shared environment? From the individuals who work for and with the organization? From customers and clients? The quarterly profit-and-loss sheet is important, but not enough for ensuring future and continuing success.

There is, whether we admit it or not, another and more basic bottom line that has to be considered along with the conventional one: the societal bottom line. The societal bottom line[16]—Mega—is basic. If you don't add measurable value to our shared world, your future is dim.

Simply look at the Fortune 500 this year and compare it to those listed in the past 10 or 15 years and see who is now missing or dropped, and then ask "Which ones didn't look after the societal bottom line?" We are in this world together. We must make money, and at the same time, add value to our shared world.[17]

Look after our shared world and it will look after you and yours. Simple. Treat others as you would have them treat you. Sensible, ethical, and practical. And as noted earlier, the concept of CSR (Corporate Social Responsibility) in general, and the observations of Davis (2005) specifically,[18] show an evolving organizational trend toward adding measurable value for external clients and society.

Three Guides for Performance Improvement

This book next presents three guides or templates to reach Mega: the Organizational Elements Model, the Six Critical Success Factors, and the Six-Step Problem-Solving Process.

The details and how-to's for each of the three guides are also provided in the referenced sources. The three basic guides should be considered as forming an integrated set of tools—like a fabric—instead of only each one on its own.[19]

Are These Guides Just Theoretical?

They are not. These are valuable lessons learned, often at great time and expense, by organizations worldwide. Think about the many organizations that have failed financially, ethically, and operationally. Most have violated one or more of the lessons provided here.

Endnotes

1. Most planning experts now agree. I first proposed using a societal frame of reference as the primary focus for individuals and organizations in 1968 and 1969 (which brought alarm and suspicion on the part of many "old paradigm thinkers"). But I have recently been joined in this call for such new paradigms by many future-oriented thinkers including (but not limited to) those included in the references in this Introduction.

    This shift in thinking to new paradigms—frames of reference that are radically different from the "conventional wisdom"—are sprouting as Joel Barker suggested they would when seen by the "Paradigm Pioneers" of our world.

2. And they all seem to keep coming...

3. System, systems...sounds at first like semantic quibbling. It isn't. Words are important. Please consider the precise and rigorous use of words and the concepts behind them as not quibbling but a potential powerful "friend" to you as you help improve our world.

4. Prahalad, C. K. (2005). *The fortune at the bottom of the pyramid: Eradicating poverty through profits.* Upper Saddle River, NJ: Wharton School Publishing/Pearson Education, Inc. This book shows examples of previously poverty trapped people in poor social and economic areas who emerged from poverty without handouts.

5. And Hurricane Katrina of 2005, an example of one of a few reactions to crisis and disaster that is characterized by splintering of authority, responsibility, and response based on conventional boundaries and not upon the health, safety, and well-being of people. Let's hope we can apply Mega to keep splinters and conventional approaches to problems as bad history and instead focus on payoffs for people regardless of what geo-political boundaries exist.

6. Based on Kaufman, R., & Watkins, R. (2000, April). Getting serious about results and payoffs: We are what we say, do, and deliver. *Performance Improvement, 39*(4), 23–32. This article provides an inclusive set of definitions for the field of performance improvement and performance accomplishment.

7. While not popular because they challenge the status quo and existing power alignments, such current ways and means of thinking, planning, and budgeting keep us from "connecting the dots" for defining and delivering societally useful results. See, for example:

Kaufman, R. (2003). What performance improvement experts must and can learn from tragedy. *2003 Team and Organization Development Sourcebook*. NY: McGraw-Hill.

Kaufman, R. (2004). War, peace, and connecting the dots: Observations about wars, missed opportunities, and what we can do about it. In Shostak, A. (Ed.). *Making war/making peace: Defeating terrorism/developing dreams: beyond 9/11 and the Iraq War, Vol. 3.* Philadelphia, PA: Chelsea House Publishers.

8. One perspective is that just looking at subsystems—jobs alone—to improve them is like efficiently and correctly rearranging the deck chairs on the *Titanic*. No matter how good that job, it still didn't prevent the collision with the iceberg. Single-issue attention.

9. Hinchliffe, D. R. (1995). *Training for results: determining education and training needs for emergency management in Australia.* Unpublished doctoral dissertation. Monash University, Clayton Campus, Victoria, Australia. This study suggests that once people are within a mindset, they find it very difficult to get out of it. The Hinchliffe study was related to the organizational elements and he found that starting people with the more comfortable inputs and asking them to move to Mega-level results were more than most people were capable of accomplishing. However, when he started them with Mega-level results, they were generally able to move from there through the organizational elements to inputs. This is contrary to the conventional wisdom of "starting people where they are."

10. Insight provided by Professor Emeritus Dale Brethower in a personal communication.

11. Based on Kaufman (1998) and Kaufman (2000).

12. Kaufman, R., & Swart, W. (1995: May–June). Beyond Conventional Benchmarking: Integrating Ideal Visions, Strategic Planning, Reengineering, and Quality Management. *Educational Technology, 35*(3), 11–14.

13. A possible criterion for your ability to be both unique and successful might be the extent to which others, no matter how misguided, come to benchmark you. Think about it: Most people do want perfection, but are afraid to commit to achieving it. But we want it. No engineer sets out to develop an average machine; they want to see how close they can get to a perfect one. The Dallas Cowboys' former coach Tom Landry noted that if you don't strive for perfection, you will never even get to excellence. In addition, the processes of continual improvement will allow us to constantly note how far we have gotten and know what to continue and what to modify.

14. Zahn, D., & Kaufman, R. (May 2005). Transformation through implementation: An idea whose time has come. *Six Sigma Magazine.* This points out that when you simply strive to reduce variability, you might just improve something that is not useful.

15. This concept comes from a reminder to me of this reality by Dr. Elizabeth Hannum of Katy, Texas.

16. Kaufman (1998, 2000); Kaufman, Oakley-Browne, Watkins, & Leigh (2003); Kaufman, Guerra, & Platt (2006).

17. Recently being touted—for reasons best known to those floating them—are additional bottom lines such as an "environmental bottom line." While it is understandable that selling something new, such as a "triple bottom line," might be good for those pushing it, it also might splinter and even fragment the concept of Mega—a societal bottom line—into subsystems and make it tempting to look at only one element of Mega and not see Mega as an integrated whole—as a fabric. Looking at an "environmental bottom line" or a "nutrition bottom line" or a "safety bottom line" might raise awareness of important parts of Mega, but it also tends to return one to fragmentation and single issue thinking, planning, and doing.

18. Davis, I. (2005, May 26). The biggest contract. *The Economist. London, 375*(8428), 87.

19. Of course, each one is valuable. But used together, they are even more powerful.

Chapter 3
The Basic Concepts and Tools
for Mega Thinking and Planning

Strategic planning focuses on the survival, self-sufficiency, and quality of life of all stakeholders. This societal frame of reference is called *Mega*. *Strategic thinking* is the mind-set behind the strategic planning process that starts with Mega. Both are essential ingredients of success.

Three Basic Guides or Templates

There are three basic guides, or templates, that will be helpful to define and achieve organizational success and to provide the rationale for useful choices.[1] Following are concepts and tools for our entry into Mega thinking and planning.

Guide 1. The Organizational Elements Model (OEM)

Figure 3.1 defines and links/aligns what any organization uses, does, produces, and delivers with external client and societal value added. For each element, there is an associated level of planning. Note that *strategic planning* (and thinking) starts with Mega, while *tactical planning* starts with Macro, and *operational planning* with Micro.

These elements are also useful for defining the basic questions every organization must ask and answer, as provided in Figure 4.2.

All Organizational Elements Are Important and Must Be Included

Each of the organizational elements are equally important. Simply because something is important to you doesn't make it "Mega." All organizational elements must be attended to and linked.

Figure 3.1: The five levels of results, the levels
of planning, and a brief description:
The Organizational Elements Model (OEM).

Name of the Organizational Element	Brief Description and Level of Focus	Type of Planning
Mega	Results and their consequences for external clients and society (shared vision)	Strategic
Macro	The results and their consequences for what an organization can or does deliver outside of itself	Tactical
Micro	The results and their consequences for individuals and small groups within the organization	Operational
Process	Means, programs, projects, activities, methods, techniques	
Input	Human, capital, and physical resources; existing rules, regulations, policies, laws	

Some Examples for Each of the Organizational Elements

In Figure 3.2 are some typical types of things you might find for each element of planning and each type of result for each level.

Figure 3.2: The organizational elements and examples of each.

MEGA	• Everyone is self-sufficient and self-reliant • Organizations (including clients and customers) are successful over time[2] • Eliminated disabling illness due to air pollution • Eliminated disabling fatalities • Positive quality of life • No welfare recipients • Continued profit over time (5 years and beyond) • Zero disabling crime • Clients' success over time (5 years and beyond) • School completer is self-sufficient and self-reliant
MACRO	• Assembled automobiles • Yearly production delivered • Goods and/or services sold • System delivered • Patient discharged • High school graduate
MICRO	• Tire • Fender • Production quota met • Completed carpet order • Completed training manuals • Competent workers • Course completed • Operation completed • Test or course passed

(Continued)

Figure 3.2 (Concluded)

PROCESSES	• Organization development • Management techniques • Operating production line • Training • Six Sigma improvement approach • Curriculum • Examining patient • Strategic planning • Assessing needs • Course development	
INPUTS	• Money • People/students • Equipment • Facilities • Existing goals • Time • Resources • Individual/values • Laws • Current economic conditions	• Regulations • History • Organizational culture • Current problems • Existing materials • Current staff and their SKAAs • Characteristics of current and potential clients • Predicted client desired and requirements

Obtaining alignment can be vital for organizational success. A useful approach is to ensure that programs, projects, policies, and activities actually complement one another. Figure 3.3 is a framework for better ensuring alignment.

Figure 3.3: Alignment table. A format for ensuring that any program or process align with all elements as well as determines its "fit" with existing policies and procedures (Column 3) as well as with laws, rules, and regulations (Column 4).

Organizational Elements (OEMS)	Program, Project, Activity	Policy, Procedure	Laws, Rules, Regulations
Mega			
Macro			
Micro			
Process			
Input			

When considering any program, project, policy, regulation, or activity, sort it into the OEM and see where it fits. Then make sure its successful completion will link and align all the elements. For example, if a training program is being considered for the production of a new toaster, that would be a process. Successful transfer of skills, knowledge, attitudes, and abilities (SKAAs) should add value to that product as it moves from within the organization to a safe and useful consumption of it. By placing it, toaster production training, in the alignment table (Figure 3.3), you may observe what is possibly missing in order to ensure linkage and to make sure that what you use, do, produce, and deliver will add value both within the organization and outside of it. An example is provided in Figure 9.4.

Of Results, Labels, and Consequences

Words, words, words. Sometimes I feel that I am witnessing a professional variation of *Alice in Wonderland* where it was said "Words mean anything I want them to mean, nothing more and nothing less." This is not exactly a good guide for planning and delivering results that involve real live human beings. We must care enough to be precise and rigorous about our words, for our words guide our actions, deeds, and consequences. For some reason, we use lots of commonly used words in what is called strategic planning and development that simply blur very important nuances. Nuances? Yes, sorry, but vital.

In common practice, people use the word *outcome* for every manner of result. They don't discriminate among results at the Mega or Macro or Micro levels. If we use the same word for all three levels of results, we will likely not align the three levels of planning.

Mega is *not* shorthand for "really big," Macro is *not* code for "big," and Micro is *not* code for "small." Mega is societal, Macro is organizational, and Micro is individual or small group. It is not about size, but rather focus. Using comfortable words might be tempting, but doing so will likely keep you from really defining and delivering success.

Figure 3.4 lists the way terms and concepts of Mega thinking and planning really work, and the way you should think about relating the three levels of planning and the three related kinds of results.

Figure 3.4: Relating planning and results.

Name of the Results—Related Organizational Element	Type of Result	Type of Planning Focus
Mega	Outcome (Mega-level results)	Strategic
Macro	Output (Macro-level results)	Tactical
Micro	Product (Micro-level results)	Operational

Why make these distinctions? Simply because when we are planning and doing, we best serve ourselves and others by being very clear about what result we should and will accomplish. Not all results are the same; there are results at each level of planning. So when someone mumbles "learning outcomes," you will make a note that they are really talking about "learning products" and they likely have failed to link the learning results with organizational results (outputs) and those to external client and societal contributions (outcomes).

Let's see this application of the meaning of the terms and concepts associated with the Organizational Elements Model in a dialog coming from your working with the instructional designer (Stan) of a training group.

Stan: We have asked people what they "need" and it is training on the generator in the central computer processing center. The "learning outcome" we are seeking through training is that the technicians will understand how the generator works and know the trouble signs.

You: Thanks for your hard work. Let me make sure I understand. We are having some problems with the generators and we want them to work better, right?

Stan: Correct. There have been generator shut downs, and they cause the computer processing center to go offline. And people inside and outside of the organization complain when that happens.

You: Let's talk about the results we want to get. Let's make sure that all of your talent really helps us all.

Stan: I told you the "learning outcomes." Anything wrong there?

You: Help me understand. The real Outcome we want is that the clients of the central computer processing center will not lose any of their money and life due to malfunction or failure, right? Doesn't our computer center support the shipment of food and drugs, and also shift money around from our organization to banks and customers?

Stan: Well, sure. But don't the technicians have to know how to troubleshoot?

(Continued)

(Concluded)

You: Of course. And they have to know what to fix and when
          to fix it. And when they make a fix, they have to double-
          check and make sure that the complete operations of
          the computer processing center serve all the clients
          properly: no spoiled and dangerous food, no spoiled or
          dangerous drugs, and no loss of financial condition that
          could harm them. Agree?

Stan: Are you saying the techs have to know more than how
          the generators work and how to spot trouble?

You: I agree, they have to know that. And they have to make
          sure that what they do and fix lead to the Outputs of our
          organization to our external clients as well as the Out-
          comes of safety and well-being of all our stakeholders.
          We have to align what the techs know, do, and com-
          plete with adding value up the line.

Stan: Well, I assume that. I guess I have to make sure that
          those aligned results really happen.

You: Again, you are right. Let me know how I might help you,
          Stan.

Analysis of this scenario: Your first clue about what Stan was
doing came when he talked about "learning outcomes." This sig-
naled that Stan was working at the individual task level (Micro-
level results/Products) and was not looking at the entire results
chain. Linking all levels of planning and results is vital.

A note on terminology: For simplicity sake, from here on out, we
will depend on your thinking in terms of the three kinds of results
and linking, not blurring, them. Success is found in linking and
relating all three levels of planning and three different types of
results. When we say "Mega results," this is code for Outcomes.
When we say "Macro results," this is code for Outputs. And when

we say Micro results, this means Products. At the end of the book, there is a Glossary of Terms.

Putting the OEM to Work

To locate what you are doing and to make sure that you realize that each of the elements is equally important *and* must be linked one with all the others, simply ask yourself "At what organizational element is this?" Remember, just because something is big or really important doesn't make it Mega.

Try the exercise in Figure 3.5 so that you can target an initiative or a condition to the OEM and locate it into the entire OEM context.

Figure 3.5: Determining organizational elements.

Condition	Mega	Macro	Micro	Process	Input
There are 112 new employees.					
Last year 3 people died from accidents caused by this item.					
Our company shipped 330 refrigerators last month.					
Training is being provided monthly.					
The rejection/re-work rate on the line last month was 7%.					
We use team management in this plant.					
New jigs and fixtures arrive in May.					
Production overall is up 8%.					

Check your answers to the exercise in Figure 3.5.

Condition	Mega	Macro	Micro	Process	Input
There are 112 new employees.					✓
Last year 3 people died from accidents caused by this item.	✓				
Our company shipped 330 refrigerators last month.		✓			
Training is being provided monthly.				✓	
The rejection/re-work rate on the line last month was 7%.			✓		
We use team management in this plant.				✓	
New jigs and fixtures arrive in May.					✓
Production overall is up 8%.			✓		

Any time you are deciding to use or do something, sort it into the OEM and thus make sure it will integrate and align with all the Organizational Elements.

Guide 2: Six Critical Success Factors

Guide 2 provides a vital framework for this approach and for Mega planning. Unlike conventional "critical success factors," these are factors for successful planning, not just for the things that an organization must get done to meet its mission. These are for Mega planning, regardless of the organization.

Guide 2: Six Critical Success Factors (CSFs) Apply to Any Organization[3]

Six critical success factors for Mega planning (not the conventional targets of one's own organizational business, but for the planning process and concern based on adding measurable value to all parties) are shown in Figure 3.6. These six critical success factors are basic guides (not tools) to help you ensure that what you use, do, produce, and deliver will add measurable value.

Figure 3.6: The Six Critical Success Factors for Mega-level strategic planning and strategic thinking (based, in part, on Kaufman [1998, 2000]).

CRITICAL SUCCESS FACTOR 1

Don't assume that what worked in the past will work now. Get out of your comfort zone and be open to change.

CRITICAL SUCCESS FACTOR 2

Differentiate between ends (what) and means (how).

CRITICAL SUCCESS FACTOR 3

Use all three levels of planning and results (Mega/Outcomes; Macro/Outputs; Micro/Products).

CRITICAL SUCCESS FACTOR 4

Prepare all objectives—including the Ideal Vision and mission—to include precise statements of both where you are headed as well as the criteria for measuring when you have arrived. Develop "smarter" objectives.

CRITICAL SUCCESS FACTOR 5

Define *need* as a gap in results (not as insufficient levels of resources, means, or methods).

CRITICAL SUCCESS FACTOR 6

Use an Ideal Vision (what kind of world, in measurable performance terms, we want for tomorrow's child) as the underlying basis for planning and continuous improvement.

These six factors are not the usual "success factors" in business books. They are not focused on one's own organization, but are broader. They are more fundamental because they are not specific to your organization or your business. Rather, they are generic: they are for any organization, public or private, to ensure what they do will add measurable value to all stakeholders.

Again, not conventional, only useful.

Guide 3: Six-Step Problem-Solving Process

A Six-Step Problem-Solving Process Model,[4] shown in Figure 3.7, in terms of results (and not the processes to deliver each result) includes:

(1.0) **Needs Assessed** that defines the gaps in results at the Mega, Macro, and Micro levels and places them in priority order

(2.0) **Needs Analyzed** that finds the causes of the needs, determines detailed solution requirements to meet the needs, and identifies (but not yet selects) solution alternatives

(3.0) **Means Selected** that involves selecting solutions from among alternatives based on the costs and consequences for the available alternatives

(4.0) **Implemented** that consists of designing and developing the means and methods that are required to meet the needs, and then putting those to work

(5.0) **Evaluated** where results are compared with the intentions (from 2.0)

(6.0) **Revisions as Required** that involves the continual improvement (at each and every step) when the required results are not being accomplished or when progress toward meeting the needs are falling short

Figure 3.7. The Six-Step Problem-Solving Process: A process for identifying and resolving problems and identifying opportunities (based in part on Kaufman [1992, 1998, 2000]).

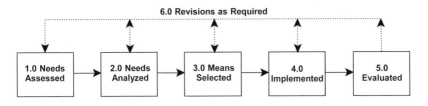

Getting from "What to Accomplish" to "How to Best Get the Job Done"

The first two functions of the Six-Step Process are primarily concerned with what to accomplish. Beginning with Step 2.0, the focus starts to shift to the details of performance system design, development, and implementation to get from where you are to meeting Mega-level needs. (Books 2 through 6 of this series provide advice on analyzing, designing, delivering, and evaluating useful results based on the prior determination of where to head.) Steps 1.0 and 2.0 in Figure 3.7 are about *what* and the balance is about *how*. The Six-Step Process is the bridge from here to there.[5]

Each time you want to identify problems and opportunities and systematically get from current results and consequences to desired ones, use the six-step process. This process model may guide you through the whole change procedure.

Using the Three Guides

These three guides form a type of tool kit for you to use as you and your organization move toward measurable success. Each time you start to do something, decide to change something, or opt to add something, "run it through" these three templates. They individually and together will provide useful decision guides.

Each time you face decisions about change or how to create change, use these:

- The Organizational Elements Model (OEM) will ensure alignment in order to allow what you use (Inputs), do (Processes), produce (Micro), and deliver outside of the organization (Macro) to make measurable contribution to external clients and our shared society (Mega).

- The Six Critical Success Factors will guide you in ensuring that what you use and do will be successful. Use all six.

- The Six-Step Problem-Solving Process will guide you as you go from needs assessment to evaluation and continual improvement.

How does this all work? Here is an application of the Six-Step Process and the other two guides based on an earlier scenario:

Stan: You mentioned a problem-solving process you use. May I walk through my approach now with you using it?

You: I am happy to review it with you.

Stan: The first thing is to assess needs. Needs, according to this process, is a gap in results. So I have to define the gaps in results, right?

You: Yes.

Stan: Your other guide was the Organizational Elements Model. According to that, when I apply the six-step process, I have to identify gaps at the Mega, Macro, and Micro levels. Those are the three levels of planning and results.

You: You got it!

Stan: The gaps in results at the Mega level are those bad things that can or could happen from the delivery of faulty food or drugs, such as sickness, permanent disability, even loss of life. I want to make sure that no

---

(Continued)

(Continued)

	needs exist or will happen as a result of our computer processing center means and operations. Next, then, I identify the gaps in results—needs—at what our organization delivers to external clients. I guess that is the Macro level. And then I determine the gaps for the individual performance level—the Micro level.
You:	Right again. Makes sense, doesn't it?
Stan:	Sure does. I was initially starting at the Micro level and assuming that closing those gaps would work for the levels above it. This way I can "prove" what results I have to get at the tech level. Then I prioritize the needs on the basis of the costs to meet them as compared to the costs to ignore them. From that I find the reasons for the gaps at the three levels and use those reasons to identify possible ways and means to close those gaps. That way I don't pick a solution, such as training, prematurely.
You:	You're right on target, Stan.
Stan:	With these data, based on performance, then I select the best ways and means to meet the needs. I do that on the basis of what it costs to do each as compared to the extent to which it will be bad if we don't meet those needs. Then I design the ways and means to meet the needs, and I guess it might not be through training if it turns out that the computer system has operating problems that it doesn't take a tech to diagnose and treat. Next I implement what we have selected, and evaluate it as we go and at the end of our efforts.
You:	And you can also constantly compare your performance and progress against those objectives and revise any time you have to. Good going, Stan, Thanks.

(Continued)

(Concluded)

Assessment: Stan walked himself right through the six-step process. It worked. Instead of starting with training and "learning outcomes," he defined needs and opportunities and saved everyone a lot of time, money, and possible grief that would have come from training that wasn't the right answer.

Further, Stan could (and should have) used the Six Critical Success Factors to ensure that he was applying the rigor required. He also could and should have formally aligned the Organizational Elements.

Endnotes

1. Each is defined in much greater detail in several books referenced at the end of this book.

2. The words *over time* are critical. Success over time indicates that what the organization delivers to external clients is safe and useful and is also reflected in continuing profits and no successful liability lawsuits against them.

3. Most "critical success factors" discussed in the management literature refer to organization-specific factors related to their unique business. The critical success factors used here are only about strategic planning itself, which will result in adding measurable value to society.

4. Earlier versions of this six-step model listed the functions in a way more compatible with the way in which system analysis (Kaufman, 2000) and flow charting should be done. This has been redesigned based on feedback in order to better communicate.

5. A note on formatting of flow diagrams: One useful way to show the order of functions—building-block products—is in a flow chart. Flow charting for strategic planning is covered extensively in Kaufman, 2000, *Mega Planning*.

Chapter 4
Mega Planning: A Choice to Define and Deliver Success

A Mega planning framework has three phases: scoping, planning, and implementation/continuous improvement. From this framework, specific tools and methods are provided to do Mega planning. It is not complex, really. If you simply use the three guides, you will be able to put it all together to define and deliver measurable success.

Mega Planning Is Proactive

Many organizations approach organizational improvement by waiting for problems to happen and then scrambling to respond—they react to problems or crises. There is a temptation to react to problems and never take the time to plan. When you elect to plan—elect to define your preferred future—surprises are fewer because success is defined before problems spring up. Then you may sensibly and systematically achieve the results you want, not the ones imposed on you.

Mega Planning Is Not Your Father's Planning Mode

What is covered here isn't that standard fare. There is ample evidence that the conventional approaches to strategic planning are not strategic (usually tactical or operational planning) and have not been wildly successful. This approach has support in application[1] and as noted earlier is picking up support from an increasing number of "main line" operations.

Figure 4.1 presents a comparison of conventional strategic planning and the Mega planning approach.[2]

Figure 4.1: Comparison of traditional and Mega planning.

Traditional "Strategic" Planning	Mega Planning and Thinking Paradigm
1. Improve the present situation. Incremental changes to the present way of doing things.	1. Strategic thinking and planning involves the design and creation of a new paradigm. It involves new techniques and skills to be successful. It often requires leaving the comfortable behind.
2. Short-term profit or funding. Objectives project from next quarter to, at most, five years.	2. Long-term objectives that design a better world for both today's and tomorrow's citizens. Make our world measurably better with no back-sliding and functional continual improvement, along with profit objectives that are 5 to 100 years plus.
3. A focus on tactics and activities not clearly connected to measurable results. Wants are often confused with needs.	3. Focuses on designing future results in measurable terms before selecting relevant strategies and tactics. Results are long term, set, and linked at three levels: Mega, Macro, and Micro.
4. Objectives define financial results only. Internal clients and future citizens are largely ignored. Positive societal impact is left to chance.	4. Objectives are designed for a balanced range of stakeholders: 4.1 Future citizens 4.2 External organizational clients 4.3 Internal organizational clients Performance indicators are chosen to define and then evaluate success and determine revisions and changes.
5. Social and environmental quality is not a formal or measurable issue in planning.	5. Societal value-added, now and in the future, is the priority issue in planning.

(Continued)

Figure 4.1 (Concluded)

6. "Needs" are defined as gaps in resources, methods, and means (e.g., we "need" more equipment, we "need" more computers).	6. Needs are defined as gaps between current and desired results. Requirement for more resources are quasi-needs and are only selected on the basis of the best ways and means for meeting the needs.
7. Level of planning focuses on immediate clients and major shareholders. Society and internal clients are not formally or rigorously considered.	7. Planning includes the integration and linking of three groups of clients: 7.1 Society now and in the future 7.2 Immediate external clients 7.3 Internal clients
8. Goals are more often general and vague, and exclude measurable criteria.	8. Objectives are SMARTER.[3] They are written for results at three levels and include measurable criteria.
9. Visions are more often short term and pertain to the organization itself and not our shared society. Organizational missions are "fuzzy" and sound good, but don't include the next generation of citizens. Societal value added is not an issue for the organization.	9. An Ideal Vision states in measurable terms the kind of world we want to cooperatively design for tomorrow's child. The organizational mission defines the contribution the organization will make to the Ideal Vision in measurable terms. Visions are about societal value added—now and in the future—not about what an organization alone wants to accomplish.
10. No shared meaning of what an organization is or must deliver. This is usually treated as a collection of unrelated parts.	10. Shared meaning on the elements common to all organizations. Systemic mental models emphasize relationship between the parts.

Finding and Justifying Direction

We can ask ourselves *Where are we headed? Why do we want to get there? How will we know when we have arrived there?* Where we choose as our destination is vital. The Organizational Elements Model (OEM) provides us with guidance on finding and justifying direction. Figure 4.2 lists the basic questions that should be asked and answered during Mega thinking and planning. These are the questions—the right questions to be asked and answered—that all organizations face. They can deal with them formally and rigorously, or they can assume them. But they are all there, all of the time.

Consider your commitment to each and all.

Which questions do you feel you and your organization can afford to avoid? Not address formally? Not link and align? The agreement table in Figure 4.3 is a way to work with, and communicate with, your internal and external partners.

What are the implications of not using and not aligning all of the organizational elements? What are the implications for not being precise, rigorous, and measurable for each and all organizational elements? Which of the questions in the finding direction table in Figure 4.2 do you think your organization *and* any of your internal and external clients can afford *not* to address formally? (This means without identifying and dealing with each in rigorous, precise, and measurable performance terms.)

Figure 4.2. The Organizational Elements Model (OEM) and the related questions that should be answered.[4]

Finding Direction
Do you commit to deliver organizational contributions that add measurable value to external clients and society? (**Mega**)
Do you commit to deliver organizational contributions that have the quality required by your external partners? (**Macro**)
Do you commit to produce internal results that have the quality required by your internal partners? (**Micro**)
Do you commit to have efficient internal processes, programs, projects, and activities? (**Processes**)
Do you commit to create and ensure the quality and appropriateness of the human, capital, and physical resources available? (**Inputs**)

Do you commit to deliver:
 	
  a. Products, activities, methods, and procedures that deliver positive value and worth?
 	
  b. The results and accomplishments defined by our objectives? (**Evaluation/Continual Improvement**)

Coming to Agreement on Mega

When doing Mega planning, you and your associates may ask and answer the questions shown in Figure 4.3, which is an *agreement table* that you can use with your internal and external partners to come to common agreement on where you are headed and why you want to get there.

Figure 4.3: The basic questions every organization must ask and answer.

Questions	Self-Assessment		Organizational Partners	
	NO	YES	NO	YES
1. Do you commit to deliver organizational results that add value for all external clients *and* society? (Mega)				
2. Do you commit to deliver organizational results that have the measurable quality required by your external clients? (Macro)				
3. Do you commit to produce internal results—including your job and direct responsibilities—that have the measurable quality required by your internal partners? (Micro)				
4. Do you commit to having efficient internal processes, activities, and programs? (Processes)				
5. Do you commit to acquire and use quality—appropriate—human capital, and physical resources? (Inputs)				
6. Do you commit to evaluate/determine: 6.1 How well you deliver products, activities, methods, and procedures that have positive value and worth? (Process Performance)				

(Continued)

Figure 4.3 (Concluded)

6.2 Whether the results defined by your objectives in measurable terms are achieved? (Evaluation/ Continual Improvement)				

A "yes" to all questions in Figure 4.3 will lead you to Mega thinking and planning and allow you to prove that you have added value—something that is becoming increasingly important. These questions relate to Guide 1 (Figure 3.1), which defines each organizational element in terms of its label and the question each addresses. If you use and do all of these, you will align everything you use, do, produce, and deliver to adding measurable value to yourself, to your organization, and to external clients and society.

If the answers by you or your partners to any of the questions in Figure 4.3 is "no," then what is offered as an alternative? If one doesn't commit to add value to internal and/or external partners, who will they add value for? If there are any "no" answers, then reasonable and better alternatives must be offered.

An agreement table is provided in Figure 4.4, and it is recommended that each person who will be involved or impacted by the plan participate and commit. Using this table and requiring actual written commitment—such as initialing each question—will help get people to understand the consequences of using and not using the approach.

Figure 4.4 provides a format to be used to actually get all internal and external partners to consider (and come to agreement on) Mega planning. It has been used in both the public and private sectors and results in (1) enlightenment ("I never thought of it this way") and (2) commitment. If some members decide not to agree with one or more items, this provides "informed consent" that puts everyone on public notice that they declined to commit to one or more of the elements of Mega planning.

The Basis for Mega Thinking and Planning—
An Ideal Vision

From asking people from almost around the world a simple question, an Ideal Vision was derived. As mentioned in the previous chapter, the question was *What kind of world do you want to help create for tomorrow's child?* The agreement was overwhelming. It coincides with what I have called *mother's rule:* Ask any mother what kind of world she wants for her children, and she will not tell you about means (budgets, funding levels, school buildings), but about basic results. None want their children murdered, raped, or permanently disabled, or to die of infectious diseases or pollution. When people are asked to define the world they want for tomorrow's child, there is great agreement.[5] The Ideal Vision—the basis for Mega thinking and planning—was provided earlier in Figure 1.1.

What is Coming: The Six Critical Success Factors
for Strategic Thinking and Planning Tools for Each

Next there are chapters that cover the Six Critical Success Factors (presented in Figure 3.6). Taken together, the Six Critical Success Factors will form critical guides to defining and delivering success. Recall that there are three basic templates, or guides, for Mega thinking and planning:

>   Guide 1: The Organizational Elements Model
>   Guide 2: The Six Critical Success Factors
>   Guide 3: A Six-Step Problem-Solving Process

Each of the chapters that follow will deal in detail with each of the Six Critical Success Factors. In the next chapter, Critical Success Factors 1 and 2 will be discussed.

Figure 4.4. A strategic thinking and planning
agreement table (from Kaufman [1998, 2000]).

Strategic Thinking and Planning Agreement Table	COMMITMENT			
	Clients		Planners	
	Yes	No	Yes	No
1. The total organization will contribute to clients' and societal survival, health, and well-being.				
2. The total organization will contribute to clients' and societal quality of life.				
3. Clients' and societal survival, health, and well-being will be part of the organization's and each of its facility's mission objectives.				
4. Each organizational operation function will have objectives that contribute to #1, #2, and #3.				
5. Each job/task will have objectives that contribute to #1, #2, #3, and #4.				
6. A needs assessment will identify and document any gaps in results at the operational levels of #1, #2, #3, #4, and #5.				
7. Human resources/training and/or operations requirements will be based on the Needs identified and selected in #6.				
8. The results of #6 may recommend non-HRD/training interventions.				
9. Evaluation and continual improvement will compare results with objectives for #1, #2, #3, #4, and #5.				

Endnotes

1. For example, the Fall 2005 issue of *Performance Improvement Quarterly* has several applications worldwide of Mega planning.

2. Based on Kaufman, Oakley-Browne, Watkins, & Leigh (2003).

3. Oakley-Browne (in Kaufman, Oakley-Browne, Watkins, & Leigh [2003]) defines SMARTER objectives as having the elements of:

S	=	Specific performance area
M	=	Measurable in ratio or interval terms
A	=	Audacious
R	=	Results focused
T	=	Time bound
E	=	Encompassing
R	=	Reviewed frequently

    This is a sharp contrast to the conventional "SMART" objectives that are self-limiting in terms of the "A" being achievable. If we only set out to do what we absolutely know we can deliver, we will never push past the comfortable here-and-now.

4. Based in part on Kaufman (1998, 2000).

5. Of course, there are always "nut cases" who seem to be self-destructive and cheering for the destruction of others. But fortunately, they are in the minority.

Chapter 5
Don't Confuse Means and Ends:
Critical Success Factors 1 and 2

Critical Success Factor 1: Don't assume that what worked in the past will work now. Get out of your comfort zone and be open to change.

There is support that just about everywhere we look, tomorrow is not a linear projection—a straight-line function—of yesterday and today. Car manufacturers squander their dominant client base by shoving unacceptable vehicles into the market. Airlines focus on shareholder value and ignore customer value. We see rapid changes coming upon us, such as leaps in telecommunications (the capacity of cell phones increasing), computer technology (yesterday's memory size and computing speed are literally dwarfed by today's capabilities, and that just seems to be the beginning), and mores and morals.

Change often comes on us quickly, frequently in huge leaps rather than "baby steps." If we try to change gradually when the change is rapid, we will always be behind reality. When change is required, you should change on the basis of data, change on the basis of knowing what results should be accomplished, and change rapidly. In most cases, slow change just makes things worse, perhaps like pulling an impacted wisdom tooth slowly.

An increasing number of credible authors have been telling us that the past is, at best, prologue and not a harbinger of what the future will be. In fact, old paradigms can be so deceptive that Tom Peters suggests that "organizational forgetting" must become conventional organizational culture.[1]

It was not so long ago that just about everyone (except for two Australian medical researchers who recently won a Nobel Peace Prize) treated ulcers as coming from stress. It turns out that ulcers come from a virus. Much earlier it was believed that the Earth was the center of the universe. There are legions of items of conventional wisdom that were (and are today) accepted by most people, including these from the past, but have, with the fullness of time, shown to have been at least incomplete if not plain wrong.[2]

Louis Pasteur's theory of germs is ridiculous fiction.
–Pierre Pachet, Professor of Physiology at Toulouse, 1872

640K ought to be enough for anybody.
–Bill Gates, 1981

Heavier-than-air flying machines are impossible.
–Lord Kelvin, president of the Royal Society, 1985

I think there is a world market for maybe five computers.
–Thomas Watson, Chairman of IBM, 1943

There is no reason anyone would want a computer in their home.
–Ken Olson, president, chairman, and founder of Digital Equipment Corporation, 1977

Everything that can be invented has been invented.
–Charles H. Duell, Commissioner, U.S. Office of Patents, 1899

Times have changed, and anyone who doesn't also change appropriately is risking failure. It is vital to use new and wider boundaries for thinking, planning, doing, and delivering. Doing so will require getting out of current comfort zones. Not doing so will likely deliver failure.[3]

As we noted earlier, Mega thinking and planning is based on an Ideal Vision and is important as the core of Mega thinking and planning. Please review it in Figure 1.1. (A shorthand version is: the survival, self-sufficiency, and quality of life of all people.)

A decision question for any choices you have to make is:

Will this choice take me closer to or further away from Mega?

If you maintain your objectivity, the answers to this question will give you very quick, rapid advice.

Quick review: If you are not adding value to the Ideal Vision, are you subtracting value? If you are not adding value to achieve the Ideal Vision, are you a short-term solution to no known overall problem? Are you just in the quick-fix, band-aids on brain-tumors business? What are the ethics of not adding measurable value to your external clients and society?

Making money and doing societal good must not be mutually exclusive. Most existing planning and performance improvement approaches do not formally start with Mega—with societal value added. Why would you choose to continue a model or process that is, at best, incomplete? One tell-tale signal that an approach is conventional and incomplete is that it has a focus on "the business case." Conventional, but obsolete.

What's wrong with making money? What's wrong with getting your public sector organization more funding? Nothing. However, no organization can do so by doing harm to our shared world. So there is a second "bottom line" for all organizations: *the societal bottom line.*

For best results, first look after the societal bottom line and the profit bottom line will surely follow. If it doesn't, your business has not been adding value to external clients and society. Mega, it is strongly suggested, is the guide to ensure that you are and will be adding value to all stakeholders. Not conventional, but it is the practical and the safest approach you can take.

There are many tools and practices that have worked before, but might not work now, especially without direct linkages to Mega. We won't go into the definitions and nature of each, but here is a list for you to consider:

- Systems Approach
- Systems Analysis
- Program Planning and Budgeting System
- Management by Objectives
- Management by Exception
- Management by Walking Around
- Total Quality Management
- Instructional Design
- Performance Improvement
- Benchmarking
- Empowered Work Groups
- Six Sigma
- Excellence
- Trust Walks
- Outward Bound

Each one of these had some merit and followers. Each has proven to be, at best, incomplete, and others only focused on a part of the organization and not on the whole and what each process, approach, or method will contribute to external clients and our shared society.

Critical Success Factor 2: Differentiate between ends and means. Focus on *what* (Mega, Macro, Micro) before *how*.

People are "doing-type critters." We want to swing right into action and in so doing we usually jump right into solutions—means—before we know the results—ends—we must deliver. Ends and means are different while being related: the only rational way to choose any means (training, development, initiatives) is on the basis of the results we are to deliver. Means should be based on the ends to be accomplished.

Almost all performance improvement authors agree on writing and using measurable performance objectives. Objectives correctly focus on ends and not methods, means, or resources.[4] Ends—*what*—sensibly should be identified and defined before we select *how* to get from where we are to our destinations. If we don't select our solutions, methods, resources, and interventions on the basis of what results we are to achieve, what do we have in mind to make the selections of means, resources, or activities?

Focusing on means, processes, and activities is usually more comfortable as a starting place for conventional performance improvement initiatives. Starting with means, for any organization and performance improvement initiative, would be as if you were provided process tools and techniques without a clear map that included a definite destination identified (along with a statement of why you want to get to the destination in the first place). If you started a performance improvement journey with means and processes, there would be no way of knowing whether your trip was taking you toward a useful destination nor would there be criteria for telling you if you were making progress.

Separating and Relating Means and Ends:
An Exercise to Sort Out Ends from Means

It is vital that successful planning focus first on results—useful performance in measurable terms—for setting its purposes, measuring progress, and providing continual improvement toward the important results, and determining what to keep, what to fix, and what to abandon. Complete the exercise in Figure 5.1 to help sort out the differences between ends (*what*) and means (*how*).

Figure 5.1: Determining ends and means.

For each item on the list below, put a checkmark in the appropriate column depending on whether it is primarily an end (results, consequence, or payoff) or a means (resources, methods, how-to-do-its, interventions, processes, approaches, methods).

	End	Means
Learning problem solving		
Looking for a job		
Having positive self-esteem		
Training		
Downsizing		
Strategic planning		
Tactical planning		
Operational planning		
Best practices		
College graduate		
Survival		
Negotiating an end to terrorism		
Six Sigma		
Assessing needs		
Benchmarking		
Continuous improvement		
Team building		
Loving		

Check your answers to the exercise in Figure 5.1:

	End	Means
Learning problem solving[5]		✓
Looking for a job		✓
Have positive self-esteem	✓	
Training		✓
Downsizing		✓
Strategic planning		✓
Tactical planning		✓
Operational planning		✓
Best practices		✓
College graduate	✓	
Survival	✓	
Negotiating an end to terrorism		✓
Six Sigma		✓
Assessing needs		✓
Benchmarking		✓
Continuous improvement		✓
Team building		✓
Loving		✓

Just because something is important doesn't mean that it is an end. Negotiating an end to terrorism is a means we all want to be successful, but negotiating is not the same as getting the terrorism to end. Similarly, training is a means to get useful competence and successful performance: an end that is useful and worthy. We should not confuse any *how* (a means) with the results or ends. One verbal cue that you might be dealing with a means is that just about all words in the English language ending with "ing" (planning, developing, training, managing, creating) are means. To find out what ends might be related, simply ask "If we were successful with this means, what would the result be?"

Are there just some things that are not measurable? Sorry, the answer is "no." We often hear statements such as "This is an 'intangible,'" or "This is a 'soft skill,'" or "That is just not measurable." Is that true?

What is true is that everything is measurable. And everything can be measured on one of the mathematical scales of measurement.

For some people, that statement might be seen as taking things too far. Everything measurable? Yes indeed. Despite our common beliefs that things are intangible or ethereal or insubstantial or "just plain not measurable" the truth is that they are, and on a mathematical scale of measurement.[6]

Following is a taxonomy of results[7] that relates scales of measurement and to demonstrate that everything is measurable.

In fact, if you can name it, it is measurable. If you can't name it, then what is it? The scale of measurement for naming is termed *nominal scale* measurement.[8]

The next most reliable scale of measurement is called *ordinal scale* measurement. This type is used in judging art (first, second, third prize) and judging livestock. It simply ranks things in terms of greater-than, less-than, or equal.[9]

Next in reliability is the one most of us think of when we hear *measurable.* But it is only one type of measurement out of four possibilities. When we have equal scale distances (such as the difference between 4 and 5 degrees) and an arbitrary zero point (temperature reported from the airport), we have measurement on an *interval scale.*[10] We use this type of measurement in educational results reporting and social statistics.

The most reliable scale of measurement is the ratio scale. It is when we have equal scale distances (such as the difference between 4 and 5 degrees) and a known zero point such as temperature in Kelvin where matter stops moving, or in distance, or weight.[11] [12]

So why all of this fuss about measurability? Only because it is vital. We must set objectives in measurable performance terms (where we are headed and how we will know when we have arrived). And everything is measurable, so don't let anyone, including you, get away with the excuse that something is "just not measurable." Measurability will make us accountable for the success we choose and will allow us to realistically check our progress.

Figure 5.2 shows the taxonomy—hierarchy—of results and the names for each.

Figure 5.2: The Four Scales of Measurement and their related purposes (based on Kaufman [1972] and Stevens [1951]).

Name of Scale of Measurement	Name of Purpose They Are Used For
Nominal	Goal (or Aim or Purpose)
Ordinal	Goal (or Aim or Purpose)
Interval	Objective
Ratio	Objective

A *goal* states where you are headed (improve my love life, get a better job, be happy, be successful, be the boss).

An *objective* states both where you are headed as well as how to measure when you have arrived (marry my soul mate within one year, within two years get a new job that earns at least 23% more than my current job).

The more you can state your purpose in interval or ratio scale terms, the more likely you are to be able to make useful decisions on how to get from here to there.

Does this rigor really make a difference? Does it make any sense to go to all of this trouble? You bet, at least if you want to get beyond mediocrity or even being wrong.

If you care enough about the consequences of a decision, then you should care enough to make sure you set your objectives in hard, objective, and measurable terms.[13] If you don't, what risks, perhaps not at first obvious, are you really taking?

Mega Planning and Doing Is Not a Linear, Rigid, or Lock-Step Approach

Relating means and ends is a dynamic—not linear, not lock-step—relationship within an organization. An end, or result, at one point in development is the beginning of a means or activity that, in turn, delivers another end. Means and ends should be linked, related, and aligned to move increasingly toward Mega. Figure 5.3 illustrates the dynamic nature of means and ends.

Figure 5.2: The dynamic nature of means and ends.

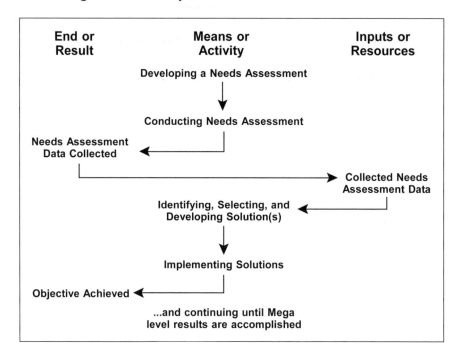

It is vital to focus on useful ends before deciding how to get things done. It also sets the stage for Critical Success Factor 3, (Use and link all three levels of results) through application of the Organizational Elements Model (OEM) and for Critical Success Factor 4 (Prepare objectives that have indicators of how you will know when you have arrived). The OEM relies on a results-focus because it defines what every organization uses, does, produces, delivers, and the consequences of that for external clients and society.

Endnotes

1. Peters (1997).

2. From Kaufman (2000).

3. Again, in Peters (1997), he states that it is easier to kill an organization than it is to change it.

4. Bob Mager set the original standard for measurable objectives. Later, Tom Gilbert made the important distinction between behavior and performance (between actions and consequences). Recently, some "Constructivists" have had objections to writing objectives because they claim it can cut down on creativity and impose the planner's values on the clients. This view, I believe, is not useful. For a detailed discussion on the topic of Constructivism, please see the analysis of philosophy professor David Gruender (1996, May–June).

    A useful aid is the "Hey Mommy Test" that was quoted in my 1998 strategic thinking book. It encourages you to take whatever purpose statement you have prepared (objective) and say, "Hey Mommy, let me show you how I can...." If it is a useful objective, it will provide a reasonable set of criteria.

5. In common English usage, if a word ends in "ing" you can count on it as a means and not an end.

6. S. S. Stevens in 1951 wrote that there were four scales of measurement. His formulation is the basis of this section on "everything is measurable."

7. Kaufman (1972). *Educational system planning.* Englewood Cliffs, NJ: Prentice-Hall.

8. There are statistics for nominal scale results: Chi Square.

9. A statistic for this is Rank Order Correlation.

10. A statistic for this includes means and standard deviations, and tools such as analysis of variance.

11. Or our bank account as this is being written. By the way, my wife tells me she is not overdrawn, but I am simply under-deposited.

12. Statistics for this are the same as for interval scale data.

13. Professor Emeritus Dale Brethower notes "if you care, get the facts."

Chapter 6
Using and Aligning the Levels of Planning and Results: Critical Success Factor 3

Critical Success Factor 3: Use and link all three levels of results.

As we noted in Critical Success Factor 2 (Focus on ends and not means), it is vital to prepare objectives that focus only on ends (or results)—never just on means or resources. There are three levels of planning and results, based on who is to be the primary client and beneficiary of what gets planned, designed, and delivered. For each level of planning, there are three levels of associated results. *Strategic planning* targets society and external clients, *tactical planning* targets the organization itself, and *operational planning* targets individuals and small groups.

Recall the linking and aligning of all organizational elements:

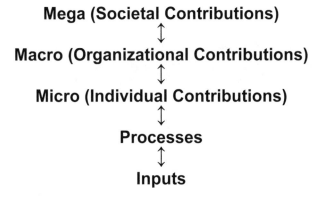

Mega (Societal Contributions)

↕

Macro (Organizational Contributions)

↕

Micro (Individual Contributions)

↕

Processes

↕

Inputs

Mega: The primary client/beneficiary are external clients and society.

Macro: The primary client/beneficiary is the organization itself.

Micro: The primary client/beneficiary is a small group or an individual within the organization.

It doesn't make much sense if you get results at the Micro level that don't add value—have positive impact—on results and consequences at the Macro level. Further, it doesn't make much sense to get results at the Macro level that don't add value to the Mega level—to external clients and society.

Yet, when we blur the three levels and even talk about every manner of results—be it at the Micro, Macro, or Mega level—by the same label we can fail to link Mega, Macro, and Micro, but this is not a good idea.[1]

Why Link and Align the Three Levels of Planning and Related Results

Completing the exercise in Figure 6.1 will demonstrate the importance of linking and aligning.

Figure 6.1: Linking and aligning planning and results.

For each of the organizational elements, identify which ones you currently do not address rigorously, measurably, and precisely and which ones you do address rigorously, measurably, and precisely:

Level of Planning and Type of Results	Do Not Address Formally and Rigorously	Do Address Formally and Rigorously
Mega		
Macro		
Micro		
Processes		
Inputs		
Continual Improvement		

1. What are the risks of starting at the Mega level? What are the risks of *not* starting at the Mega level?

2. In what ways are you adding value to your organization? To your external clients? To our society/community? What could you be doing and contributing?

Attending To and Aligning All the Organizational Elements

Consider this in terms of using and aligning all three levels of planning and results (Mega, Macro, Micro). If you get results only at the Micro level, are you adding value to your organization and external clients?

The exercise in Figure 6.2 shows the planning/results lineup. Which ones do you formally attend to? Which ones will you attend to in the future?

Figure 6.2: Determining attention to planning and results.

Level of Planning and Results	Primary Focus	Example	Do you formally attend to this now?	Which one(s) will you formally attend to in the future?
Mega	Society, external clients	"Arrive alive"; zero deaths from terrorism; zero harmful pollution		
Macro	Organization	Customer satisfaction; quarterly profits		
Micro	Individual or small group	Mastered training objectives; competent performer		
Process	Activities, training, doing	Training, facilitating, development, time for training		
Input	Resources—human, capital, physical	Hired associates, funds, policies, values		
Evaluation and continual improvement	Fixing, improving, never blaming	Quality management, Six Sigma		

Figure 6.3 provides a job aid—an algorithm—to use to ensure that your objectives target ends and that they align with all three results areas:

Figure 6.3. An algorithm for objectives and ensuring their linkage at the three levels of planning and three levels of results (based on Kaufman [2000]).

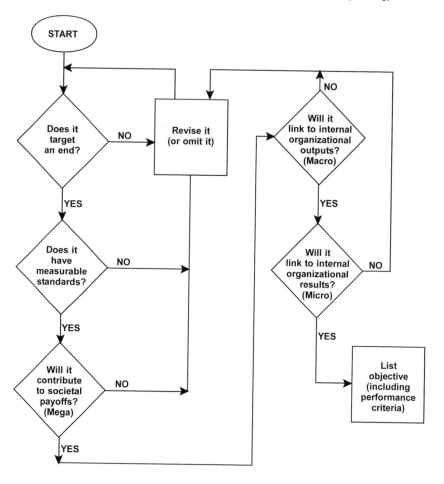

Ensuring Linkages

Getting the linkages and ensuring the alignment among the organizational elements, are very vital. If there are disconnects between Micro results and Macro results, and disconnects between Macro results and Mega results, success is not likely. Imagine developing a training program for call center staff that meets all of the Micro level performance requirements but results in lost customers. Linkage and alignment can mean the difference between success and failure.

One way to check the alignment is to ask, at each level of results—Mega, Macro, and Micro—the following question:

Does this Mega level result provide useful guidance for defining Macro level results?

Keep asking that question over and over through each of the organizational elements: Mega to Macro to Micro to Processes to Inputs.

When you are checking from within the organization to determine the linkages and viability of internal organizational efforts and contributions, ask:

- Will this Input allow required processes to be developed and implemented?

- Will this process deliver the required results at the Micro level?

- Will these Micro level results deliver the required Outputs?

- Will these Macro level results deliver measurable value added for external clients and society?

Alignment starts with Mega and rolls down to Macro to Micro then to Processes and then to Input. The strategic thinking and planning sequence is illustrated in Figure 6.4.

Figure 6.4: The roll-down flow of strategic thinking
and planning and the relationships and linkages among
Mega, Macro, Micro, Processes, and Inputs[2]

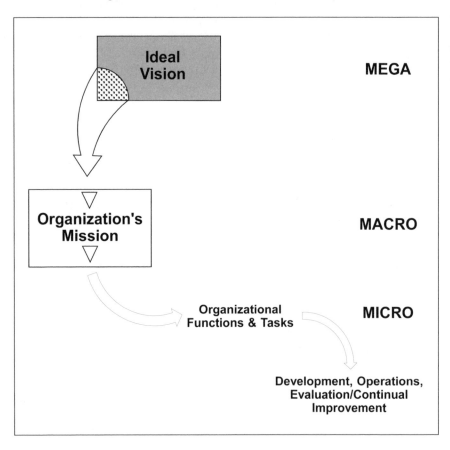

This is an "outside-in" process where you start strategic thinking and planning at the external client/societal level and roll down to
make sure that what you do, develop, and deliver will add value all
up and down the value chain: the value chain of the linked organizational elements.

What are the implications of this choice? Simply, everything
you develop and deliver will add value internally and externally and
you will be able to prove it. This is not of minimal importance.

Change Management and Change Creation[3]

Change Management

In order to survive, every organization must respond—react—to change thrust upon it by changed realities. Reaction to change—*change management*—is vital. There is extensive literature on this topic. Change management requires quick and nimble responses to defining and managing change. If an organization only uses change management, it can limit them from defining useful change before being overtaken by it.

Change Creation

At the same time as the reactive responses to change are operating, there is another parallel cohort of organizational success: *change creation.* This is appropriate for any organization that realizes that it must be proactive and not wait for the impact of overtly imposed change: one must create the future and not just react to it.

Reacting to change and creating the future are both vital and must be part of any strategic, tactical, and operational planning and implementation.

In order to not just survive but also thrive, the organization identifies and creates the changes that will be required for a successful future. *Change creation,* while dignifying *change management,* moves beyond it while dignifying its importance. Both operate in parallel.

It is very difficult to predict the future. So what should the approach be to dealing with tomorrow? Management expert Peter Drucker (1985) advises that if you can't predict the future, create it.[4] This "creation of the future world we want to create for tomorrow's child" is the essence of *change creation* as well as Mega planning. Mega planning uses an Ideal Vision as the shared destination for all organizations (Figure 1.1). *Change creation* enrolls the organization to define and achieve a shared and mutually useful future that relates all an organization uses, does, produces, and delivers to add value to external clients and society: Mega planning.

Change creation is the proactive process whereby an institution and its people:

1. Describe, in measurable terms, the future they want to define, design, and deliver.

2. Accept, invite, and welcome change as a vital component to achieve future success.

3. Create the designed future and continuously improve it while moving ever closer to the desired future: the Ideal Vision.

In this approach, the desired future is defined, justified, and designed by all partners. Then a transition plan to create the designed future is developed and implemented. When *change creation* is energized, an organization and its people consciously move from being victims of change to partnering with and mastering change.

Change management is a fact of life. As unpredicted changes occur, they must be met and used to improve one's survival. Simply reacting to change will not allow an organization to thrive; it will simply just survive.

Both surviving and thriving mean taking genuine responsibility for leading change, effectively planning for the desired change (i.e., strategic planning), and developing and implementing a change approach that capably transitions people, processes, and circumstances from what exists to the shared desired future. A comparison of change creation and change management is provided in Figure 6.5.

Figure 6.5. A comparison of change creation
and change management.[5]

Change Creation	Change Management
Proactive	Reactive
Be benchmarked	Benchmark others
Setting the standard	Trying to be competitive
Leading	Following
Long view	Quick fixes
Vision-driven to add value to all stakeholders	Driven by external events
Internal planning for a better future	Externally imposed disruptions
Change-adaptable/Change-inviting mindset: A learning organization	Responsive mindset
Create change	Expect more change
Mega-level strategic planning	Tactical planning and operational planning
Aligns strategic, tactical, and operational planning	Confuses and fuses operational, tactical, and strategic planning
Focuses on all of the organization plus external clients and society	Focuses on parts of the organization
Requires change-champion executives and sponsorship	Requires change-responsive executives and sponsorship
Performance improvement initiatives linked to Mega payoffs	Training initiatives
Thrive	Survive
Increased effectiveness, efficiency, and value added	Increase efficiency

(Continued)

Figure 6.5 (Concluded)

A "system" approach	A "systems" approach
Focus on external clients and society linking to organizational mission	Focus on organizational mission or business needs
Encourages ownership of change	Accounts for individual stress of change
Works to reinvent a new corporate culture	Works within the current corporate culture
Transformations	Fixes
Continuous improvement toward "perfection"	Continuous improvement of current functions and tasks
Stability in motion	Disruptive instabilities
Welcome and create seamless change	Accept and expect change
Future-creating organization	Responsive and resilient organization
Outside-in/top-down planning	Inside-out/bottom-up planning
Society as well as organization as beneficiary	Organization as beneficiary
Long-term effectiveness	Short-term effectiveness
Learning organization	Organizational learning
Long-term profit/funding	Quarterly profit/funding
External opportunity finding	Environmental scanning

There is no distinct choice between change management and change creation. Both are important. Scan the entries in Figure 6.5 and identify the extent to which you and your organization might add the usually missing change creation to its strategic thinking, strategic planning, operations, evaluation, continual improvement, and culture. The proactive change creation approach is really aligned with Mega thinking and planning. By simply reacting to change—change management—one is always responding, catching up, and not really taking control of creating one's own future.

Endnotes

1. Why different labels for different levels of results? It is not conventional. Most writings in performance improvement use "outcome" for *any* kind of result. This book urges that you think and act on the basis of three different levels of planning (and the three levels of results that were defined in Chapter 3).

2. Based on Kaufman (1998, 2000).

3. These concepts extend the work of Kaufman & Lick (2000) and Lick & Kaufman (2000) and other related publications on this topic as well as a presentation to the ISPI Change Conference in Washington, D.C., November, 2000.

4. .And it is widely agreed that we cannot really accurately predict the future.

5. Based on Kaufman, R., & Lick, D. (Winter 2000–2001). Change creation and change management: Partners in human performance improvement. *Performance in Practice,* 8–9.

Chapter 7
Prepare Objectives that are Really Useful: Critical Success Factor 4

Critical Success Factor 4: Prepare objectives to include precise statements of both where you are headed as well as the criteria for measuring when you have arrived.

It is vital to state—precisely, measurably, and rigorously—where you are headed and how to tell when you have arrived.[1] Statements of objectives must be in performance terms so that one can plan how best to get there, how to measure progress toward the end, and how to note progress toward it.[2]

Objectives at all levels of planning, activity, and results are absolutely vital. And everything is measurable, so don't kid yourself into thinking you can dismiss important results as being "intangible" or "non-measurable." It is only sensible and rational to make a commitment to measurable purposes and destinations. Organizations throughout the world are increasingly focusing on Mega-level results.[3]

Figure 7.1 shows that there are differences between goals and objectives and that regardless of the level—Mega, Macro, Micro—they all should be rigorous and measurable.

An organization might set the following goal: "Improve the profits of our organization." Adding interval or ratio-scale criteria to this goal might create the following objective: "Increase profits by at least 10% a year for five consecutive years." The goal notes "where the organization is headed," and the objective precisely adds to that "how the organization knows when it has arrived." So no matter whether you are preparing objectives for the societal/Mega level, for the organizational/Macro level, or for the individual performance/Micro level, you should be precise and rigorous: state measurably where you are headed and how you can tell when you have arrived.

Figure 7.1: The relationship and characteristics
of goals and objectives.[4]

Where are you headed? and How will you know when you have
arrived?

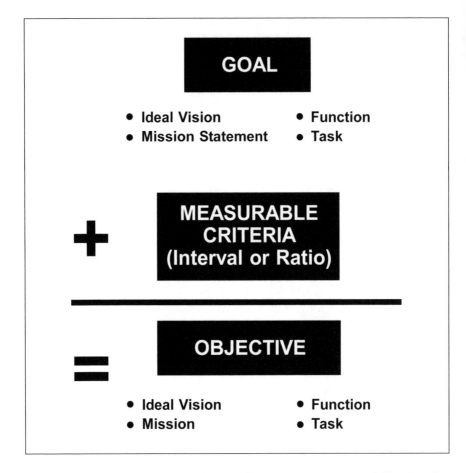

To check on your relating ends, means, measurability levels,
and the organizational elements, use Figure 7.2 to see where you
are relative to all of this. It is an activities progression.

Figure 7.2: The relationship among ends and means, reliability of measurement, and organizational element focus.

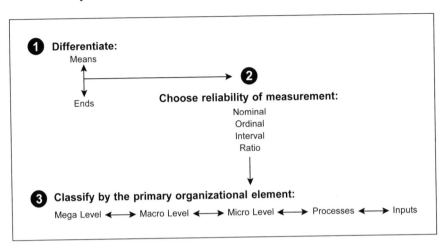

We have been moving along in defining where we should head, why we should get there, and the importance of measurable rigor. Let's turn our attention now to some guides and tools to use as you think and apply Mega.

A Guide for Choosing a Societal, Community/External Client-Focused Result

Beginning with the result (or objective you have chosen), the OEM table in Figure 7.3 shows a Mega approach to achieving a result.

Figure 7.3: OEM table: Mega approach.

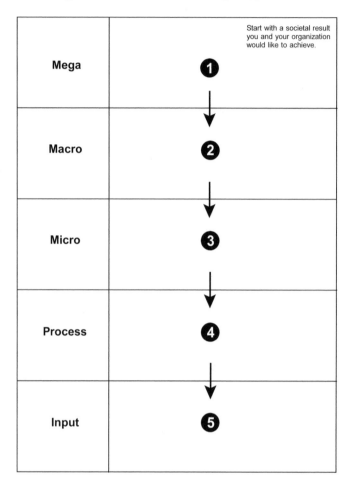

If you are working on an existing organizational program or context, the upward and more conventional flow is presented in Figure 7.4. Note that this "inside out" approach is what is usually done. It is not very often that people get to Macro or Mega results and consequences, so they miss the assurance that what they use, do, produce, and deliver will add value to all internal and external stakeholders.

Figure 7.4: Traditional approach.

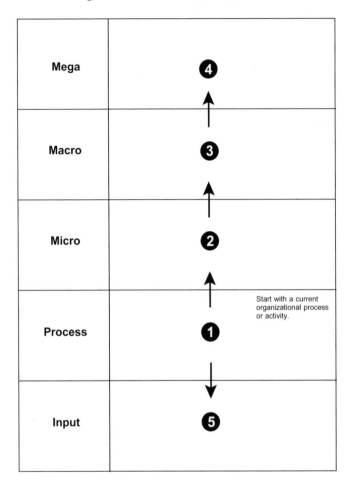

When starting "inside" their organization or their operational assignments, most people quickly get stuck in their comfort zones and never make the full alignment.[5]

Exercise for Ensuring Linkage and Alignment with Mega

You might want to consider a practical and *ethical* perspective-adjustment by using similar questions to those in the previous exercise to evaluate yourself and your organization. Complete the exercise in Figure 7.5 with regards to your current assignment or organization. For Column 2, list actual related objectives that actually demonstrate impact on the health and safety of all clients. In Column 3, note intended results at each of the three planning and results levels where health, safety, and welfare are not the priority. This exercise will let you know if what you intend to do and deliver is or is not linking to measurable external value added.

The Mission Objective and Its Relation to Mega

The mission objective states, in measurable performance terms, the results the organization will deliver as it moves ever closer to meeting the Mega level needs selected for closure. Figure 6.4 provided the "roll-down" relationships between Mega, Macro, and Micro results, and this relationship is useful so that you always relate the levels of contributions for each level of results.

Mission Objective

Based on the Mega level needs to be fulfilled, the mission objective can be derived by the planning team. Here is a simulated mission objective:

> *Any future storms in the catchment area will result in zero loss of life for residents and visitors in the area; zero disabilities; no losses of income for individuals, organizations, or governments, infrastructure, buildings; no losses from criminal behavior; zero damaging flooding from levee failures and pump failures; no evacuees will be gone for more than 24 hours and will return to safe and secure dwellings.*

Figure 7.5: Alignment with Mega exercise.

Your Organization and Your Job	The health, safety, and welfare of all clients is the priority	The health, safety, and welfare of all clients is NOT the priority
The Mega level results* achieved by your clients and society when using that which is delivered by you and your organization		
The Macro level results** delivered outside of your organization		
The Micro level results*** you create		
The Processes and activities you do		
The Inputs and resources you use		

   *   Outcomes
  **   Outputs
*** Products

This example mission objective provides both direction—what results must be delivered—as well as hard criteria for planning and measuring success.

Next, the planners and performance improvement team can identify gaps between current ability to meet these mission-level requirements and the required performance (including critical elements such as building, equipment, facilities, resources, humans, etc.).

From these gaps, alternative methods and means could be identified, such as strengthening the levees, storm-proofing buildings and shelters, performance-based funding, etc.

Next, the building block functions, or products, can be displayed in a flowchart to show the results that have to be accomplished to get from What Is to What Should Be.[6]

Endnotes

1. An important contribution of strategic planning at the Mega level is that objectives can be linked to justifiable purpose. Not only should one have objectives that state "where you are headed and how you will know when you have arrived," they should also be justified on the basis of "why you want to get to where you are headed." While it is true that objectives only deal with measurable destinations, useful strategic planning adds the reasons why objectives should be attained.

2. Note that this Critical Success Factor also relates to Critical Success Factor 2.

3. Kaufman, Watkins, Triner, & Stith (1998, Summer).

4. Based on Kaufman (1998, 2000).

5. Hinchliffe, D. R. (1995). *Training for results: determining education and training needs for emergency management in Australia.* Unpublished doctoral dissertation. Monash University, Clayton Campus, Victoria, Australia.

6. The methods and concepts for developing mission profiles and detailed system analyses are provided in Kaufman (1998 and 2000).

Chapter 8
Correctly Defining Needs (Not Wants):
Critical Success Factor 5

Critical Success Factor 5: Define *need* as a gap in results (not as insufficient levels of resources, means, or methods).

Need is NOT a verb! Conventional English-language usage would have us employ the common word *need* as a verb (or in a verb sense) to identify means, methods, activities, and actions and/or resources we desire or intend to use.[1] Terms such as *need to, need for, needing,* and *needed* are common, conventional, and destructive to useful planning. What?

As hard as it is to change our own behavior (and most of us who want others to change seem to resist it the most ourselves!), it is central to useful planning to distinguish between ends and means. (We have already noted this as Critical Success Factor 2.) In order to do reasonable and justifiable planning, we have to (1) focus on ends and not means, and thus (2) use *need* only as a noun. *Need,* for the sake of useful and successful planning, is only used as a noun—as a gap between current and desired results—as illustrated in Figure 8.1

Figure 8.1: A need (as a noun) is a gap between current results and required results (from Kaufman [1998, 2000]).

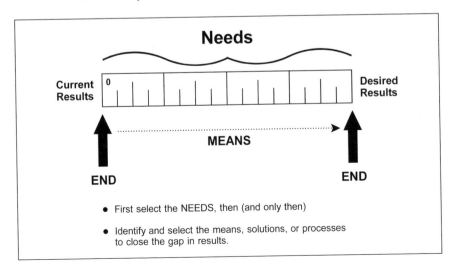

If we use *need* as a noun, we will be able to not only justify useful objectives, but we will also be able to justify what we do and deliver on the basis of costs-consequences analysis. We will be able to justify everything we use, do, produce, and deliver. It is the only sensible way we can demonstrate value added.[2]

Needs, Nouns, Verbs, and Conflict

Many arguments, conflicts, and misunderstandings are because common language uses *need* as a verb, such as "We need more time," "We need more money," "We need to economize," "We need to outsource," "We need to reorganize." Thus, people unthinking or unknowingly jump into solutions before defining and justifying a problem. (A *problem* is a need chosen for reduction or elimination.)

By jumping into a solution—a means, method, intervention, technique, or tool—by using *need* as a verb, the arguments can begin! We can argue, if arbitrary power isn't inserted, almost end-lessly about which means is better if we don't define what gap in results a means will close. To reduce conflict as well as selecting solutions-in-search-of-problems, simply go back to basics: first define the needs (as gaps in results) and then consider and select the means to close those gaps in results.

Definitions

A *need* is a gap between current results and desired or required results: a noun.

A *needs assessment* identifies the gaps between current and desired results (best including needs at the **Mega**, Macro, and Micro levels) and places them in priority order on the basis of the costs to meet the needs as compared to the costs to ignore the needs.

A *problem* is a *need* selected for elimination or reduction.

Needs are not Wants, and Means are not Ends

Understand that everything that is called a *need* or a *needs assessment* really might not be a real need or needs assessment. Following is an exercise that can help sort out what *needs* and *needs assessments* are.

Blurry Worldwide Industries: A hypothetical case study[3]

Here is a hypothetical example of the results of a needs assessment done by Blurry Worldwide Industries:

**Blurry Worldwide Industries
Needs Assessment Summary**

1. We have to have everyone managing with vision.

2. We need to be world-class.

3. We have to be competitive.

4. We need more executive development and training.

5. We need to cut production cycle time.

6. A need exists to make quality our first priority.

7. We must all work together as partners.

8. We must increase our production by 18%.

9. There must be no deaths or disabling injuries from what we deliver.

10. We must make a net-net-net profit each and every year.

11. We must not bring harm to living things.

12. We need to use performance technology.

---

1. Examine each of the above "needs assessment" statements and identify which elements of each:

    *   Identify a **need** as a gap in results.

    *   Identify a **quasi-need:** a "need" as a gap in methods or a gap in resources.

2. For each need identified, classify it as:

    > **Mega**/Outcomes-related
    > **Macro**/Outputs-related
    > **Micro**/Products-related

Based on what you find in this exercise:

3. For each quasi-need, ask "If I did or delivered this, what result would I get?" Keeping that question until you have identified needs at the three levels of results, list them.

4. Review an existing "needs assessment" and identify if it is likely to be useful and appropriate. If the reviewed "needs assessment" does not meet the basic criteria, what changes to it should be made?

Let's compare answers:

1. *We have to have everyone managing with vision.*
    The word *managing* is the key here: it is a means (Process). It states nothing about what results and payoffs there will be from "managing with vision" nor does it state what the vision will be.

2. *We "need" to be world-class.*
    This aspiration never defines what "world-class" is or how we would measure it. It also does not state what the results and payoffs will be from being "world-class." If we don't know current results, we cannot determine if there are gaps between that and whatever "world-class" means. This does not relate to a need, but is an intention, and a blurry one at that.

3. *We have to be competitive.*
This aspiration never defines what "competitive" is or how we would measure it. It also does not state what the results and payoffs will be from being "competitive." This does not relate to a need, but is an intention, and—like #2—another blurry one.

4. *We "need" more executive development and training.*
This is a means. Your first clue that it is a means is the use of *need* as a verb, which dumps one into means—executive development and training—without defining the ends to be accomplished. In this case, what gap in results would be closed by "more executive development and training"? What gap in results would this deliver at the Mega, Macro, and Micro levels?

5. *We "need" to cut production cycle time.*
This is also a means. Your first clue again is the use of *need* as a verb, which dumps one into means—reducing production cycle time—without defining the ends to be accomplished. In this case, what gap in results would be closed by "cutting down on production cycle time"? What gap in results would this deliver at the Mega, Macro, and Micro levels?

6. *A "need" exists to make quality our first priority.*
Again, this is a means. Your clue is the use of *need* in a verb sense—limiting means without defining the ends to be accomplished. In this case, what gap in results would be closed by "making quality our first priority"? What *is* "quality" and how do we measure it? What gap in results would this deliver at the Mega, Macro, and Micro levels?

7. *We must all work together as partners.*
This is also a means; work together is a process. In this case, what gap in results would be closed by "working together as partners"? What gap in results would "working together" deliver at the Mega, Macro, and Micro levels?

8. *We must increase our production by 18%.*
    At last, a result at the Micro level. If it were stated as a
    "need"—a gap between current results and desired ones—
    it might be stated: "Current production is at X and we will
    increase it to at least Y, an increase of production of at
    least 18%." It is interesting that this one doesn't also spec-
    ify that there will be no increase in rejections; one could
    increase production by the amount requested while making
    rejections and re-works increase by 125+%.

9. *There must be no deaths or disabling injuries from what we
    deliver.*
    This will deliver results at the Mega level. If stated as a
    need, it might read "Last year there were three disabling
    injuries and one death from our Outputs. Next year and
    following there will be no disabling injuries and no deaths
    from our Outputs."

10. *We must make a net-net-net-profit each and every year.*
    This will deliver results at the Mega level to the extent to
    which profit is earned without bringing harm to anyone or
    the environment. Profit over time is an indicator of a Mega-
    level contribution. If stated as a need, it might read "Last
    year we had a loss of $2.23 million. Next year—and fol-
    lowing—we will increase our profits by at least 5% every
    year." This one is a bit tricky: Profit alone would be Macro,
    but since it is continual each and every year, it is an indi-
    cator of doing no harm to external clients and society. For
    if harm were done (death, toxic disabling pollution, fraud,
    etc.) the profits would likely be reduced or even thrown into
    an operating loss.

11. *We must not bring harm to living things.*
    This will deliver results at the Mega level to the extent to
    which what the organization does and delivers does not
    bring harm to the environment and living things; they are
    "good neighbors." If stated as a need, it might read "Last
    year we had two spills cited by the environmental council
    for being toxic and destructive; next year and each and
    every year following, we will have no incidents causing
    toxic damage or other kinds of destruction."

12. *We "need" to use performance technology.*
    Performance technology is a means, even though it could
    be a very powerful means if used at the right time with the
    right people under the correct conditions.

Ask, "If we were successful at using performance technology,
what would the results of that be?"

Also, notice that *none* of **Blurry Worldwide Industries'**
"needs" were stated as gaps in results. This is a common mistake,
and one you can avoid. Also, notice how many times *need* was
used as a verb ("We 'need' to use performance technology") and
thus moving anything the organization uses, does, and delivers
toward a focus on solutions rather than results and value-added.

So making sure you use *need* as a noun—as a gap in results—
is vital to define where you are headed and justify why you want to
get there.

Working with Needs as Gaps in Results

Here is a format for recording needs for each of the organizational
elements:

Based on the discussion of the Organizational Elements Model
(OEM), please complete Figure 8.2 with examples that apply to
your personal and/or professional life (your choice of which one).

Figure 8.2: A table for recording needs (gaps in results)
for each of the organizational elements.
(Note that only the first three are ends.)

	What Should Be	What Is
Mega Results		
Macro Results		
Micro Results		
Processes		
Inputs		

Need is an over-used word. The way it is conventionally used leads to means before defining and justifying the ends to be accomplished. People confuse needs and wants (ends and means) all the time. And the consequences of getting these confused are not pretty. Ever hear a family member say things like:

> *I need new shoes.*
> *I need a new car.*
> *I need a new dress/suit.*
> *I need to go to the mall.*
> *I need more allowance.*
> *I need more money.*
> *I need...*

Well, you get the idea. They use *need* as a verb so that it takes away your (and their) choices. When one uses *need* as a verb, it is very demanding: no options, no choices, just the solution (more money, new car) that they have pre-selected. Thus, people are constantly picking solutions before they know the problems.

Just about anything gets called a "needs assessment." Most of the time, what they are really doing and using is a "wants assessment" because they are asking for processes and solutions that are desired. As an example of the confusion, a popular method in literature (and indeed popular in practice as well) is a "training needs assessment." If you believe the writings of Deming[4] and Juran[5] and if you do training needs assessment, you will be wrong 80 or 90 percent of the time.

Why? Each of these noted professionals contend that 80 or 90 percent of all breakdowns are not individual performance (Micro/Products) breakdowns, but systems (Macro or Mega) breakdowns. So if you only fix something—no matter how well or how cleverly—at the individual performance level (through such interventions as training, performance technology, job aids, electronic performance supports), then you will only be right a very small percentage of the time. You can spend a lot of time, effort, and money at the Micro/Product level, but if the breakdowns are above this level, then you have wasted many resources and probably frustrated the people involved. Read the following case study for an example.

A U.S. government agency learns the hard way about needs assessment versus wants assessment:[6]

The phone rang about 11:15 a.m. It was a nice day here, but the person on the other end identified himself and his agency and noted some frustration. I was asked, "Can you help us on a needs assessment problem?" and I answered, "Perhaps." The conversation went like this between me and the government supervisor of needs assessment for his federal agency:

Supervisor: Doc, we have a problem with our recent needs assessment and want your help.

Me: Let's see what the situation is and what I might contribute.

Supervisor: We have a couple of rooms full of needs assessment data and we can't seem to make any sense of it.

Me: Don't tell me, let me guess. You sent out a questionnaire and asked people "what they need."

Supervisor: Yes, that is exactly what we did. And it went out to thousands of our agency people worldwide. And most of them responded. But we can't make any sense of their responses.

Me: I am going to give you some bad news. Not only won't you be able to make much sense of it, but when you sent out the assessment, there was an implicit promissory note that you were going to meet their needs.

Supervisor: Why can't we help the people in our agency who told us about their needs?

(Continued)

(Continued)

Me:	Because you asked them about "needs" in terms of solutions, means, resources, and assistance—actually "wants"—so now you only have data dumps about means and what they want you to give to them. In your well-intentioned assessment, you confused ends with means, and without data about any gaps in results and consequences, you can't rank order or prioritize. What is going to happen is that the physicians are going to go to international meetings and you won't have any money left for bandages and medicines. When there is a results-vacuum, you get the organizational "golden rule": those with the gold make the rule. Sorry, but there is little hope sorting out your responses into something you can use and justify any decisions that you make.
Supervisor:	What do you mean? That sounds pretty harsh.
Me:	Look, "needs" are sensibly defined as gaps in results, not gaps in resources or activities. You can't prioritize means along without gaps in results to link them with because you can't calibrate the costs of meeting the "need" as compared to the costs for ignoring the "need." You have harvested "wants" and not needs.
Supervisor:	Oh #@%%$! What do I do now?
Me:	I would look at possible patterns in the "wants" and see if you can sense what gaps in results they might have gone with. And you might want to call together a representative sample of your associates and ask them to identify the gaps in results at the individual performance level

(Continued)

(Concluded)

	(Micro), the organizational contributions level (Macro), and the external client and societal level (Mega) and use that as a rough guide.
Supervisor:	I can't do anything with my current data?
Me:	Nothing that will lead to useful decisions and help all your agency's associates. And next time, define *need* as gaps in results, not as means or wants.
Supervisor:	I am in trouble. I thought I was getting the best advice around concerning needs assessment. And now I see the flaw in our thinking and actions.

Assessment: Once again, the conventional wisdom about *needs* and *needs assessments* were wrong, and expensive. Define *need* as a gap in results and *needs assessments* as the harvesting of gaps in results at the Mega, Macro, and Micro levels and placing them in priority order based on the costs to meet the *needs* as compared to the costs to ignore the *needs.*

Three "Bonuses" for Using Need as a Noun

There is a "3-for-1 sale" for using *need* as the gap in results between current results and consequences and desired results and consequences:

1. The What Should Be criteria serve as your measurable objectives—your performance criteria—for specifying where you are headed and how to tell when you have arrived. Successful performance design and development require us to state our objectives in measurable performance terms, ideally on an interval or ratio scale. Defining *need* in this way yields such objectives and they are based on actual performance.

2. The gaps between current results (What Is) and desired/required results (What Should Be) provide the basis for sensible, sensitive, and justifiable evaluation. That is a positive bonus, which comes from using *need* as a noun.

    Usually we get told, "We don't have the time and/or resources for evaluation," and this answers that invalid objection to doing evaluations. (Interesting how some people don't have the time or resources to do an evaluation, but have to come up with them when an intervention or program fails.)

    By using *need* as a gap in results, one only has to plot the extent to which performance results have migrated from the previous What Is to the What Should Be. The extent to which the gap in results has been reduced or eliminated is the evaluation—evaluation based on performance data.

3. Using *need* as a noun allows you to justify where you are headed, why you want to get there, and what the payoffs are for doing so. It provides an almost "bullet-proof" rationale for any proposed work or activities.

    Most proposals get turned down because they cost too much, there is not enough time, or there are not enough resources. This negative decision may be made if the proposal was based on the cost to meet the needs— the cost to close the gaps in results.

    Now the third bonus for defining *need* as a noun: When you collect solid data on the gaps (best at the Mega, Macro, and Micro levels), you may price out (a) the costs to meet the needs, and (b) the costs to ignore the needs. This is a major difference with conventional approaches to proposing programs, projects, or activities.

If you provide the decision maker with both the costs to meet the needs as well as the costs to ignore the needs (think about the costs for not having safe oil tankers, for not having non-rollover cars, for not having safe food or medicines) and they decide not to go ahead with meeting the needs you have specified based on valid data, they become accountable for not meeting the needs.

When estimates of *costs-consequences* (based on Mega and needs assessment as defined here) have been accomplished, there is a solid base for decisioning.[7] Applications have varied from industry to state government, including the Florida Division of Blind Services, Refinor (Argentina), international poverty, State of Ohio Workforce Development, Australian architectural company, to name a few.[8]

What would a typical "big-picture" case look like?

A Not-So-Hypothetical Example:
Costs and Consequences for a Major U.S. City[9]

A major U.S. southern city is below sea level, or at least 80 percent of it is. Weather experts have noted that it is not a matter if a major hurricane will hit it, it is a matter of when. For years, the city mothers and fathers have not seemed to have paid serious attention to the levees that protect much of the city. Proposals to the federal government have been under-funded for over 20 years. The feds didn't trust the U.S. Army Corps of Engineers, and the government didn't trust the state and local authorities and boards to actually use (rather than skim), funds to meet specifications, and the citizens became isolated from the real and possible dangers. National and much local emergency response to crises was primarily focused on terrorism and on-the-ground law enforcement. But life in this city and area went on for many years, dodging hurricane bullet after hurricane bullet. The luck was counted on to continue.

Then a category 4 monster hit east of the city (some later readings put it at a possible category 3 or even a category 2 when it hit the affected area, a level that the levees were supposed to withstand). The next day, flooding covered the vulnerable 80 percent and evacuations were crippled due to poor planning, bad logistics, and no leadership from the mayor and governor, or from the federal government that came in later, after much loss of life, human misery, and looting. Name calling and blame placing began immediately.

(Continued)

The mayor blamed the feds, as did the governor, and the mayor and governor pointed fingers at each other. Some said that the levees, designed to withstand a category 3, failed even though the hurricane might have been a category 2 when it hit the city. Did the levees fail due to poor engineering or poor maintenance? Were the levees built in pieces and hunks that didn't match one with the others and thus provided an invitation to failure?[10] When was evacuation called for and when was it made mandatory? What local transportation was enlisted to evacuate the poor, unlucky, and unfortunate? When was martial law declared? Who called out the National Guard, and when? Were some of the police actually "virtual police" who were hired on the Federal Safe Streets funding—police who were on the payroll, but never appeared on the streets? Who requested federal aid, and when. Who decided on aid and when? Where was FEMA and were they ready to act? Was rescue inhibited by location, weather, and natural barriers? Who was unprepared, incompetent, scared, or limited by laws?

Was it worth counting on luck? You decide. One estimate of costs for the U.S. Army Corps of Engineers to construct the proper water safeguards, if allowed by the various local and state officials, was around $500 million. The costs, rough of course, from the burden on those displaced, on our economy, and to rebuild the city is about $100 to $200 billion.

What was the cost of not meeting the need (gaps between survival of the city and citizens and the costs of loss of life, buildings, and lives)? About $150 to $200 billion. And what were the projected costs to avoid those gaps? About $500 million. The difference might be seen in terms of opportunity costs—what else could have been done with the $500 million in hopes the "big one" would not come? What else could the $500 million have been spent on that would have had an equal or greater return on investment?

What criteria were decision makers using, and what criteria might have served them and us all? Were they using Mega results criteria or Macro, Micro, Process, or Input criteria?

(Continued)

(Concluded)

This issue is about decisions based on costs and consequences: The costs to meet the needs as compared to the costs to ignore the needs. This case is Mega-focused (or in this case, not Mega-focused). And was this a case of everyone "doing their own thing"—a systems approach—and no one looking at the entire societal requirements and well-being—a system approach? What are the implications of a focus on the splinters of our world—neighborhoods, cities, counties, states, commissions, local law enforcement agencies, fire departments, Homeland Security, Reserves, sheriff departments, welfare agencies, charities, boards, elected politicians, rules, regulations—without a shared focus on the survival, self-sufficiency, and quality of life for residents? Who is in control in an emergency? Who is in control for planning for emergencies? Our current systems approach to our world leads to fragmentation, ineffectiveness, inefficiency, and grief. One U.S. senator publicly proclaimed "there was a failure at all levels of government." All.

At least two lessons might be imbedded here: (1) there were no costs/consequences assessments made before, during, and after the tragedy, and (2) there was fragmentation of attention and responsibility.

Can we learn from this and change what has to be changed? What are the rewards for change as compared to the rewards for just tinkering with the structure and mind-sets that exist?

Time will tell what really happened and what should and could have happened. The point here is that applying Mega thinking and planning could have saved many lives, many dollars, and perhaps avoided much human misery.

Change, choices, consequences.

Estimating costs and consequences is covered later in the chapter on pages 128 through 130.

Estimating costs and consequences is covered later in this chapter on pages 125 through 129.

Needs at the Mega Level[11]

Using the not-so-hypothetical example earlier in this chapter, let's explore needs as gaps in results. Figure 8.3 provides a partial table to show needs as gaps in results.

Figure 8.3: Needs—gaps in results.

What Is	What Should Be/Could Be
1,000+ people dead	0 dead or injured
$100 billion plus property damage from storms	$0 property damage from storms
27,000 displaced people with no jobs or sources of income	• 0 displaced people • All residents self-sufficient and self-reliant
X miles of polluted city with severe health hazard potential	• 0 pollution • 0 health hazard from pollution
Income loss to government of $Y	$0 loss of government income from natural causes (e.g., storms)
Z looters arrested and in jail from citizen, public, and business loss of property; no fraud with suppliers or volunteers	• 0 criminality • 0 losses from illegal activity
Flood damage to levees making them dangerous for future storms	No vulnerability from future storms of flooding
Medical supplies and medical treatment not available for immunization and de-contamination, resulting in permanent and disablement of residents	No reduction of self-sufficiency and self-reliance based on lack of response, medical supplies, and treatment
Etc.	

For each element at the Mega level, there are gaps in results identified. These are all related to Mega results and consequences. Not practical or real-world? Just put yourself in the shoes of those impacted by storms and see if these gaps in results should not be closed. Can we achieve closure for all? We ethically have to see how close we can get in the future.

Needs, Needs Assessment, and Evaluation: Related yet Different

Because this concept is so vital to successful planning and performance improvement, we will present the definitions and review the terms.[12]

Definitions

- *Need:* A gap in results—a gap between current results (and consequences) and desired or required results and consequences. It is always used as a noun, never as a verb. No gap in results, no needs.

- *Needs assessment:* The collection of gaps in results—ideally at the Mega, Macro, and Micro levels—and placing them in priority order on the basis of the costs to meet the needs as compared to the costs of ignoring the needs. (More on this later.)

- *Quasi-need:* A gap in Inputs—resources and ingredients—or a gap in Processes—means, methods, programs, projects, activities. It relates to gaps in means and resources, not gaps in results.

- *Problem:* A need selected for reduction or elimination.

- *Ends:* Results, contributions, accomplishments, Products, Outputs, Outcomes.

- *Means:* Methods, resources, processes, procedures, how-to-do-its, activities, programs, projects, interventions.

(Continued)

(Continued)

- *Wishes* (or wants): Preferred or valued means.

- *Evaluation:* The result of comparing your intended results (and consequences) with your actual results (and consequences). Evaluation is always reactive—after the fact.

- *Mega-level planning:* Planning that views the society and community, now and in the future, as the primary client and beneficiary of what gets planned and delivered.

- *Macro-level planning:* Planning that views the organization itself as the primary client and beneficiary of what gets planned and delivered.

- *Micro-level planning:* Planning that views an individual or small group as the primary client and beneficiary of what gets planned and delivered.

- *Mega-level results* (Outcomes): The social impact and payoffs of results. Mega level of planning results, such as individual self-sufficiency, individual self-reliance, collective social payoffs, continuing profits over time, continuing funding for a public sector organization, etc.

- *Macro-level results* (Outputs): Results that can, or are, delivered outside to external clients (including society). These are results at the Macro level of planning. Examples could include a delivered computer system, delivered service to a customer, a finished house, etc.

- *Micro-level results* (Products): Results that are building-blocks for larger results (test score, course passed, game won or lost, disk drives produced, etc.). They are the results at the Micro level of planning. A Product could be a completed transmission, the skills acquired in training, a completed e-learning course, etc.

(Continued)

(Concluded)

- *Processes:* The methods/means/media/activities used to deliver a result. Examples might include the how-to-do-its, such as training, organizational development, HRD, computer-assisted instruction, managerial procedures, using a balanced score card, Six-Sigma programs, etc.

- *Inputs:* The ingredients, or starting conditions, under which one is expected to or will have to operate, such as laws, values, rules, regulations, existing personnel, and resources, etc.

- *Organizational elements:* The results and ingredient elements that every organization has and uses: Mega, Macro, Micro, Process, and Input.

The Basis for Useful Results and Consequences

The basis for planning serves as the criteria for design, development, implementation, evaluation, and continual improvement. It is vital that everything any organization uses, does, produces, and delivers is driven by valid results. And these results are gleaned from a valid and appropriate needs assessment.

The use of rigorous and useful tools for determining needs and objectives will be vital in dealing with change, choices, and consequence.

Needs assessments are the basis for establishing validating goals and objectives based on performance data. Because the objectives are based on the gaps in results and the costs to meet the needs as compared to the costs to ignore them, a needs assessment allows one to identify and justify any objectives. Rather than relying on judgment, intuition, precedents, or authority, needs assessments provide the direction and justification for:

1. Where you are headed

2. How you know when you have arrived (performance criteria for evaluation)

3. Why you want to get there

Providing such performance data is not only sensible, but it is safe—a good basis for choice and decisioning.

How Your Organization Goes About Planning

Figure 8.4 lists some considerations for you and your organization to calibrate how you go about planning (and the implications for the basic concepts of Mega planning).

Figure 8.4: Calibrating how your organization goes about planning.

Rarely, if ever	Almost Never	Not Usually	Quite Frequently	Consistently	WHAT IS ← / WHAT SHOULD BE →	Rarely, if ever	Almost Never	Not Usually	Quite Frequently	Consistently
					Describe how you see yourself currently operating. / Describe how you think you should be operating.					
					1. Plans on the basis of the identified needs (as gaps in results)					
					2. Plans on the basis of ends					
					3. Plans on the basis of consequences of results for external clients					
					4. Plans on the basis of consequences of results for society and community					
					5. Plans only on the basis of individual performance					
					6. Plans only on the basis of resources					
					7. Plans only on the basis of activities, programs, projects					

(Continued)

Figure 8.4 (Continued)

Rarely, if ever	Almost Never	Not Usually	Quite Frequently	Consistently	← WHAT IS WHAT SHOULD BE →	Rarely, if ever	Almost Never	Not Usually	Quite Frequently	Consistently
					Describe how you see yourself currently operating. Describe how you think you should be operating.					
					8. Plans only on the basis of desired individual results					
					9. Plans on the basis of small group results					
					10. Plans on the basis of departmental or section results					
					11. Plans on the basis of organizational results					
					12. Plans on the basis of results for external clients					
					13. Plans on the basis of results for society and community					
					14. Plans to link resources to activities, programs, projects					
					15. Plans to link resources to results that add value for clients and clients' clients					
					16. Chooses means and resources (e.g., training, restructuring, layoffs) without first identifying results to be achieved					
					17. Defines and uses needs assessment for identifying gaps in results for impact on external clients and society.					
					18. Defines and uses needs assessment for identifying gaps in results for impact on the organization itself (such as a business plan)					
					19. Defines needs assessment for identifying gaps in results for impact on individual operations or tasks					

(Continued)

Figure 8.4 (Concluded)

Rarely, if ever	Almost Never	Not Usually	Quite Frequently	Consistently	WHAT IS ← Describe how you see your-self currently operating.	WHAT SHOULD BE → Describe how you think you should be operating.	Rarely, if ever	Almost Never	Not Usually	Quite Frequently	Consistently
						20. Rank orders needs on the basis of the costs to meet the needs as compared to the costs of ignoring them, using Evaluation Data					
						21. Links organizational results to external consequences (i.e., results for clients and clients' clients)					
						22. Uses data from a needs assessment to set objectives					

Using the Results of "How We Plan"

The statements in Figure 8.4 provide some clues concerning whether or not Mega thinking and planning are being used. The following items are vital for functional planning and meeting the Critical Success Factors. Check yourself and your associates and see what changes you might consider.

If you are doing the most useful kind of planning, you will have positive responses to all of the following items in Figure 8.4: 1, 2, 3, 4, 9, 10, 11, 12, 13, 14, 15, 17, 18, 19, 20, 21, and 22. Especially important are 1, 2, 3, 4, 12, 13, 15, 17, 20, 21, and 22.

The other items target internal and limited frames of reference. If you have positive responses to items 5, 6, 7, 8, and 16, your frame of reference for planning is probably too narrow and restrictive and you will likely focus only on parts of organizational performance and not the total fabric of it.

Start the dialog about useful planning and use the Six Critical Success Factors (Figure 3.5) to guide you.

A Needs Assessment Work Guide

It has already been noted that when a useful needs assessment is done:

- Needs are defined as gaps in results, not gaps in resources (Inputs) or processes/activities/solutions (Processes).

- There are three levels of results—Mega, Macro, and Micro levels[13]—and thus there are three levels of needs assessment.

- Needs are linking among the three levels of planning and results.

- A *quasi-need* is a gap, but not a gap in results. They are gaps in Inputs or Processes.

When identifying needs (as, of course, gaps in results) they are best in interval or ratio scale terms (see Figure 5.2). The more precise and rigorous you can sensibly be, the better your chances of getting useful results.

Asking the Right Questions for Any Needs Assessment

Five Types of Needs-Assessment—Related Questions[14]

Any menu of needs assessments should include useful options that will answer important performance questions. Following are some questions that provide alternative frames of reference (or units of concern) that a needs assessor and/or evaluator may address:

Results-Related:

Type 1: "Are you concerned with the usefulness (impact and payoffs) of what your organization will deliver to external clients and our shared society?" This is a Mega-level focus.

Type 2: "Are you concerned with the quality of what your organization will deliver outside of itself?" This is a Macro-level focus.

Type 3: "Are you concerned with the quality of what an individual or a small group within your organization will produce?" This is a Micro-level focus.

Processes and Resources-Related:

Type 4: "Are you concerned with the efficiency of the methods and procedures that will be used by an individual or a small group?" This is a Process-level focus and is actually a *quasi-needs assessment* because while it looks at gaps, the attention is to gaps in Inputs and Processes, not with gaps in results.

Type 5: "Are you concerned with the availability and/or quality of resources that will be used by an individual or small group?" This is an Input-level focus.

It should be noted that these types must be linked, and all must be present and related.

A Needs Assessment Guide, or Algorithm

Figure 8.5 is a job aid for doing a needs assessment and making sure that needs are linked and aligned at all levels of planning and results. You may use this when you want to affirm that your needs assessment will be appropriate and useful.

Figure 8.5: A job aid for ensuring that a needs assessment considers and links all three levels of planning and results.[15]

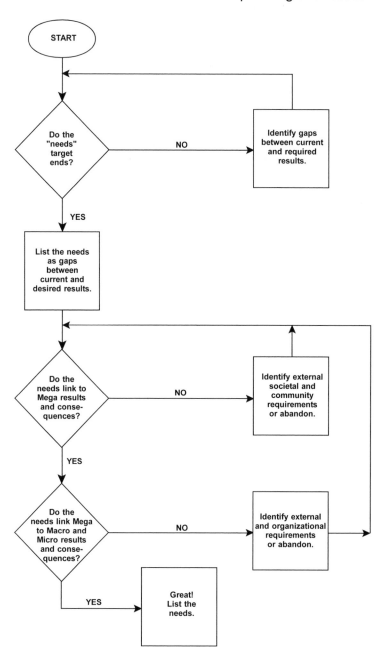

Hard and Soft Data[16]

There are two kinds of data to be collected. Both are important and useful:

- *Hard data:* Independently verifiable
- *Soft data:* Personal and not independently verifiable

Hard data can be collected in many ways and from many sources. We can go to organizational records and public records. We can get data on sales, returns, production rates and rejects, absences, complaints, etc. There is a lot more data available from public and internal sources than most people at first realize.

Soft data may be collected with questionnaire, inventories, interviews, and meetings.

Tips on Developing a Needs Assessment Questionnaire

Sometimes it will be useful to develop a needs assessment questionnaire, so following are some guides in checklist format for deriving a useful one:

❏   1. Make certain that the questions are about **results,** not about processes or inputs.

❏   2. Ask about perceptions of gaps in **results** for both dimensions—what is and what should be.

❏   3. Ask questions about the three levels of needs:

- External contributions (Mega)
- Organizational contributions (Macro)
- Building-block internal and operational results (Micro)

❏   4. Have evidence of appropriate validity and reliability of the questions and the sample.

❏   5. Make the questionnaire long enough to get reliable responses, but short enough that people will actually respond.

❏   6. Use an approach that makes it clear to respondents exactly what is wanted. People usually don't want to write long answers, so a checklist or multiple-choice format will reduce their burden while making the questionnaire easier to score.

❏   7. Don't ask questions that reveal, directly or indirectly, a bias. Don't use the data-collection vehicle to set up the responses you really want.

❏   8. Ask several questions about each dimension or issue. Ask about each concern in different ways, to increase the reliability of responses. Basing any decision on answers to one question is risky.

❏   9. Try out the data-collection instrument on a sample group to identify problems in meaning, coverage, and scorability. Revise it as required. This step is the same as the sixth step in the problem-solving model (continual improvement).

When collecting performance (or hard data):

❏ 10. Make certain the data collected relate to important questions for which you want answers.

❏ 11. Assure yourself that the data are collected correctly and that the methods used for gathering it and reporting it are free of any bias.

❏ 12. Assure yourself that the data are based on enough observations to make them reliable, not a one-shot happening.

❏ 13. Make certain that the data can be independently verified and cross-checked.

Having the data from this will be basic to your evaluation where one compares obtained results with intentions.

Evaluation—Different Yet Related to
Needs Assessment[17]

Needs assessment and evaluation are related but not the same. Let's take a look at how they are related, how they are different, and how both are key to successful planning and doing:

- Needs assessment and planning are proactive; they seek to define and achieve a useful future.

- Evaluation is reactive; it finds what worked and what did not.

- Evaluation is after-the-fact. Needs assessment and planning are before-the-fact.

- Evaluation data should be used *only* for fixing and improving, *never* for blaming.

- The basics of evaluation are not complex, but you might think so from the literature and all the "cult followings" and rituals.

- Evaluation data: Comparing "what was accomplished" with "what was intended" is best used for continual improvement. *Continual improvement* is the process for changing what should be changed whenever you realize that a change is required.

- Evaluation should use two kinds of data: hard and soft. Hard data is independently verifiable, and soft data is personal and based on perception. Make sure that both kinds of data agree.

- Needs assessments should also include both hard and soft data, but these data only relate to finding the gaps between current results and desired ones.

- When Mega is considered in evaluation, it is called "Evaluation Plus" to indicate that it goes beyond conventional evaluation frameworks.

Needs Assessment vs. Evaluation

Both needs assessment and evaluation deal with gaps, but for different purposes. When you *evaluate,* you compare, after-the-fact, the results that were obtained with the results you intended to accomplish: a comparison of what was accomplished with what was intended.

When you do *needs assessment,* you are, before-the-fact, finding the gaps between current results and desired ones: a comparison of What Is with What Should Be or Could Be. Evaluation is reactive; needs assessment is proactive.

Evaluation and needs assessment pose different, yet related, questions. Both compare intended with actual results, but evaluation is always after-the-fact—comparing results with intentions— while needs assessments proactively identify the gaps between current results and desired results.

Needs assessment data provide the criteria for evaluation, and evaluation provides the data about what was actually accomplished and delivered. Because the two are related (and often confused in conventional usage), let's take a closer look at the "relative" of needs assessment: evaluation. Figure 8.6 presents a tool for evaluation and continual improvement.

Figure 8.6: A job aid for deciding on what to do for evaluation and continual improvement.

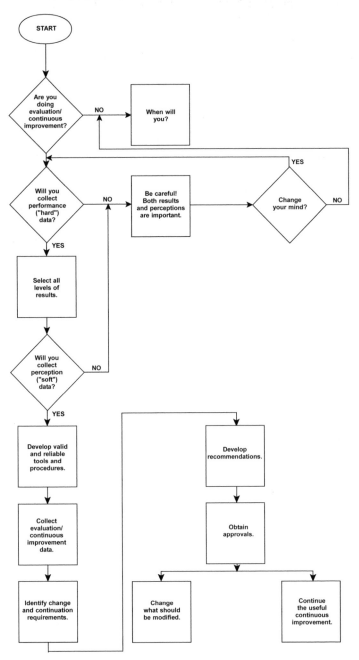

Evaluation-Related Questions

Because both needs assessment and evaluation examine gaps in results, another type of question is often asked relating to the value or effectiveness of an intervention, or the extent to which required results have been achieved. Such reactive questions are:

> *Type E(valuation):* "Are you concerned with how well we met our objectives?
>
> and/or
>
> "Are you concerned with the value of the methods and resources that were used for getting required results?
>
> *Type A(ssessment):* "Are you concerned with identifying and justifying your goals, objectives, aims, and purposes before accepting the existing ones?"

You may wish to ask any, some, or all of the five needs assessment-related questions from page 122 as well as those for evaluation. All of these questions lurk—waiting to be asked and answered, even if we don't currently recognize them—in every organization.

None of the five questions are more "right" than the others, although each has a particular usefulness. The holistic (or Mega) planning option would be a linked chain of all the questions, flowing from Type 1 through Type 5. The smart executive manager will ask, and answer, all the questions, including the Type E ones and Type A one above.

Some Technical Considerations

Needs assessment, as defined here, is a planning process for (a) identifying the gaps between current results and required/ desired ones, and (b) placing those needs (gaps in results) in priority order on the basis of the costs to meet the needs as compared to the costs to ignore them. Since a *need* is defined as a gap in results, then there are three types of needs: one each for gaps for *Mega-level results, Macro-level results,* and *Micro-level results.*[18] Gaps in non-results, *Processes* and/or *Inputs,* are termed *quasi-needs.*

You can do needs assessment at the Mega, Macro, or Micro level by identifying gaps in results for each.

Interestingly, much of what practitioners are advised to do that gets called needs assessment, needs analysis, training needs assessment,[19] and the like, is usually *quasi-needs assessment,* because it deals with gaps in processes (e.g., training, job aids, methods of supervision, resources desired) and not with results.

By identifying correct and important needs before implementing any process or solution, you can improve your effectiveness and efficiency. Securing the necessary information for "selecting the right job" in order to do the job correctly will be fruitful. Often, when dealing with an ongoing system, evaluation data can supply you with the What Is data, but it cannot give you the What Should Be.

Proactive and Reactive Tools: Needs Assessment and Evaluation

Needs assessment is a *proactive* planning tool and is distinct from evaluation. Evaluation is a retrospective, or after-the-fact, concern with gaps between what was achieved through our efforts and the targets we have previously set for ourselves.

Needs assessments are forward looking and determine gaps between our current results and those we *should* obtain. Needs assessments are not limited to existing objectives, but may be used in deriving new ones:

- Evaluation compares results with intentions.

- Evaluation is after-the-fact. Needs assessment and planning are before-the-fact.

- Evaluation data should be used *only* for fixing and improving, *never* for blaming.

- The basics of evaluation are not complex, but you might think they are from the literature and all of the "cult followings" and rituals.[20]

Applying Needs Assessment Data Collection and Application to an Entire Organization

When a *need* is defined as a gap between current and desired/required results, this allows for some important applications: doing an organizational assessment of needs. When applying needs assessment to a large organization, the gaps in results may be determined for each of the planning/results areas: Mega/ Outcomes, Macro/Outputs, and Micro/Products as seen in Figure 8.7.

By collecting needs data for the three levels of results, one can identify the gaps that exist, prioritize each, and then use this to define gaps and areas for organizational improvement. When the gaps exist at the Mega level, then changes could be considered for the Macro, Micro, and then Processes and Inputs levels. This would allow for the alignment and linking that is required for choosing organizational success based on Mega thinking and planning.

Also, using this schema, one might easily see that any gaps in results at below the Mega level must be linked and aligned with the levels above. The nature of the organizational system—starting at Mega—is vital, and this framework helps everyone see the overall context for thinking, planning, doing, delivering, and evaluating.

Figure 8.7: The Organizational Elements Model is arrayed on two levels—What Should Be and What Is— and may be used to diagnose organizations.[21]

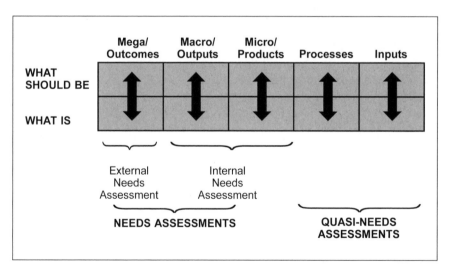

To use with an organization as a kind of "organizational analysis," use the two-tiered framework in Figure 8.7 and sort the data concerning gaps in results into the proper boxes. When you get the data inserted, you can see what is missing (empty cells or incomplete data) and if the data link from Mega to Macro to Micro to Process to Input. You will also be able to note where there are disconnects and problems.

Costs and Consequences[22]

An important bonus for using *need* only as a noun is that you may derive a reasonable set of indicators for return on investment: estimating what you give and what you get. This is very useful, because you will likely be required to justify everything you use, spend, and deliver on the basis of the costs to you and the consequences of what you deliver. It is difficult to take into account all of the possible costs and the various kinds of consequences, but you can estimate them closely enough to justify what you use, do, produce, and deliver, and to track your costs and returns.

Using an Indicator of Mega-level Consequences[23]

As noted earlier, an estimate of the societal impact—Mega-level consequences—is that an individual's consumption should be equal to or less than one's production:

$$C \leq P$$

...where C is consumption as indicated by dollars/money expended by an individual, and P is production as indicated by dollars/money obtained by an individual.

This indicator is an approximation of Mega-level consequences and payoffs, and it is based on a shorthand definition of Mega-level results that no person will be under the care, custody, or control of another person, agency, or substance as indicated by $C \leq P$.

Among the questions a costs-consequences initiative should answer are:

1. Who are the participants in the interventions? Who should be?

2. Who are being turned down for the interventions? Who should be?

3. What interventions are the participants receiving? What alternative interventions might they receive?

4. What are the results of the intervention or interventions (at the Mega, Macro, and Micro levels)?

5. What are the completion, drop-out, and continuation rates for the participants?

6. What are the performance levels of the completers? What value do they add? What about those who do not complete?

7. What is the societal condition—their levels of self-sufficiency, self-reliance, and quality of life—of the completers? The non-completers? What are the levels of completer's and non-completer's self-sufficiency and self-reliance (in terms at least of $C \leq P$)?

8. What interventions and patterns of interventions are making the best contributions in terms of societal (Mega) payoffs and consequences? What is working and what is not? What are the valid criteria for these?

9. What are the societal (Mega) payoffs and consequences for the various interventions for the various kinds of participants (in terms at least of $C \leq P$)?

10. What are the costs for the payoffs and non-payoffs, and are they worth the expenditures as compared to other interventions that might be made?

11. Have the decisions made not generalized past the completeness and quality of the data?

Exercise in Costs and Consequences

Here are two possible projects:

A. Pick a city or area of your choice that might be vulnerable to a natural disaster, then:

1. Identify the Mega-level objectives for that area.

2. Compare those Mega-level objectives to any disaster or readiness plans that exist.

3.   Identify current or potential gaps in results between what would result under the current approaches and your Mega objectives.

4.   Prioritize the gaps in results (needs).

5.   Identify detailed requirements for meeting the objectives under various threat possibilities.

6.   Identify possible ways and means to overcome or neutralize the disaster threats.

7.   Identify the advantages and disadvantages of each identified way and mean to overcome or neutralize the disaster threats using Mega as the primary criteria.

8.   Select the methods and means.

9.   Design, develop, and implement the means.

10. Prepare an evaluation and continual improvement plan that could be used during implementation if things "went wrong."

11. Start "politicking" to get your Mega plan adopted.

B. Pick an issue of great importance to your community, such as health care or crime, and then:

1.   Identify the Mega-level objectives for that issue.

2.   Compare those Mega-level objectives to any existing programs, projects, activities.

3.   Identify current or potential gaps in results between what would result under the current approaches and your Mega objectives.

4.   Prioritize the gaps in results (needs).

5.   Identify detailed requirements for meeting the objectives under various social, economic, and political possibilities.

6.   Identify possible ways and means to overcome the associated threats.

7.   Identify the advantages and disadvantages of each identified way and mean to overcome or neutralize the associated threats using Mega as the primary criteria.

8. Select the methods and means.

9. Design, develop, and implement the means.

10. Prepare an evaluation and continual improvement plan that could be used during implementations if things "went wrong."

11. Start "politicking" to get your Mega plan adopted.

The concepts and tools for Mega thinking, planning, needs assessment, and associated success can be generalized to private and public sector situations. The common underlying fabric—people, survival, and quality of life—are all present.

In making sensible and justifiable decisions, solid performance-based needs assessments that include Mega/societal consequences will provide the hard performance data required to make a solid case for change. If turned down by those in charge, the decision maker becomes responsible and becomes responsible in the face of hard data. This is a chance that most people don't want to take.

Using Costs-Consequences Analysis in Any Organization

Using the OEM and the concept of costs-consequences, the following questions help identify what was missing for useful evaluation and continual improvement to occur:

1. What data exist?

2. What data do not exist?

3. What are critical data required by the project/intervention to determine effectiveness, efficiency, and positive costs-consequences?

4. What organizational elements data exist?

5. What organizational elements data are not complete and valid?

6. Are the gaps between What Is and What Should Be identified?

7. Are all the organizational elements linked? (Does a "flow" from element to element exist and is it justified?)

Why do this? Simply because if and when you are required to report on return on investment (I prefer costs-consequences), this provides some guidelines for demonstrating "what you give" and "what you get" for actual or potential interventions.

Endnotes

1. Of course, a dictionary will tell you that it can be used as a verb. Be warned, however, when you do use it as a verb or in a verb sense, you risk jumping into solutions before knowing the real problems—confusing means and ends. The interesting thing about dictionaries is that they give "common usage," not necessarily precise or useful usage. Semantics and words are important, so please give consideration to the specific words and concepts used in this book: the precise use of words is important, even when at first it all seems like semantic quibbling. It is not. Because most dictionaries provide common usage, not necessarily correct usage, they note that *need* is used as a noun as well as a verb. This dual conventional usage doesn't mean that it is useful. Much of this book depends on a shift in paradigms about *need.* The shift is to use it only as a noun and never as a verb or in a verb sense.

2. What about Maslow and his 1964 widely revered "Hierarchy of Needs"? Actually, using terms as defined here, Maslow's Hierarchy is actually a "hierarchy of motivators"; it identifies the rough order in which an individual will be motivated to close gaps, from survival to self-actualization. These are not really needs, but rather motivators.

3. Each of these was mined from published so-called needs assessments. Based on Kaufman (1998, 2000).

4. Deming, W. E. (1982). *Quality, productivity, and competitive position.* Cambridge, MA: Center for Advanced Engineering Study, Massachusetts Institute of Technology.

5. Deming, W. E. (1986). *Out of the crisis.* Center for Advanced Engineering Technology. Massachusetts Institute of Technology, Cambridge, MA.

    Juran, J. M. (1988). *Juran on planning for quality.* New York: The Free Press.

6. The instance is real. Only the name of the federal agency has been omitted to protect the parties involved.

7. Kaufman et al (1997); Kaufman (2000); Muir et al (1998).

8. Special issue on Mega, Kaufman & Bernardez (Eds.) (2005). *Performance Improvement Quarterly, 18* (3).

9. http://www.nationalgeographic.com/ngm/0410/feature5, http://www.finfacts.com/irelandbusinessnews/publish/article_10003122.shtml

10. Some reports noted that different parts of the same levee were constructed on different specifications depending on what agency was responsible. This is a good example of a system<u>s</u> approach and not a system approach: each responsible agency looked at their part of the levee as the total system and not a subsystem of a larger system.

11. This is not complete and is only provided to offer an example.

12. A complete glossary is included at the end of the book.

13. Please recall that the associated levels and labels for results for Mega, Macro, and Micro are Outcomes, Outputs, and Products.

14. These are based on material from my books *Strategic Planning Plus: An Organizational Guide* (1992), *Strategic Thinking* (1998), and *Mega Planning* (2000).

15. Based on Kaufman (1998, 2000).

16. Again, Ingrid Guerra's book on evaluation, number six in this series, covers this and other related data collection and assessment tools, concepts, and techniques extensively.

17. Evaluation is covered extensively by Guerra in the sixth book of this series.

18. These three types of results, unfortunately, are not often distinguished in our literature. You would think that "If you've seen one kind of result, you've seen 'em all."

19. Please notice that in my list of important definitions, "training needs assessment" wasn't there. I believe that this is a misnomer for a "training requirements analysis," which is very important **after** you know that training (or some intervention) is required. After all, *training* is a means. Why would you want to do a needs assessment (determining gaps between current results and desired ones) if you already know that you are going to do training? Again, even the label of one of our favorite tools supplies a bias toward means (training) while assuming that useful ends will surely follow.

20. Evaluation based on this Mega approach is the subject of a book in this series by Guerra (2006).

21. From Kaufman (1998, 2000).

22. This section is based on Kaufman (1998, 2000) and Kaufman, Oakley-Browne, Katkins, & Leigh (2003).

23. Interestingly, most return on investment models and procedures leave out Mega. They might reach to customer satisfaction and "contributions," but do not deal with adding measurable value to both external clients and our shared society.

Chapter 9
Using an Ideal Vision for All Planning and Doing: Critical Success Factor 6

Critical Success Factor 6: Use an Ideal Vision as the underlying basis for planning and continuous improvement.

This is another area that requires some change form the conventional ways of doing planning. When people write, they use "vision," "mission," and "destination" as if they were the same. They are related, but not the same.

We have already introduced the Ideal Vision and Mega in Chapter 1 and are giving some more detail here to help you apply it. As a review, here is an Ideal Vision that is based on asking people from around most of our world, "What kind of world do you want to help develop for your children and grandchildren—for tomorrow's child?" Recall, also, that this Ideal Vision is appropriate for any and all organizations in our world: public, private, government, military, non-governmental organization (NGO). Every organization should intend to add measurable value to the Ideal Vision. Each organization chooses what elements of the Ideal Vision they commit to add measurable value to and move ever closer toward. Please review Ideal Vision in Figure 1.1.

An Ideal Vision is never prepared for any one organization, but rather identifies the kind of world we want to help create for tomorrow's child. In reality, every organization—public and private—has the same Ideal Vision. Thus, each and every organization are means to societal ends. Each organization is responsible for adding measurable value to our shared communities and society. The elements of the Ideal Vision an organization commits to deliver and move ever closer to become the organization's **mission.**

From this societal-linked Ideal Vision, each organization can identify what part or parts of the Ideal Vision it will commit to deliver and move ever closer toward. If we base all planning and doing on an Ideal Vision of the kind of society we want for future generations, we can achieve strategic alignment for what we use, do, produce, and deliver, and the external payoffs for our Outputs.

Using an Ideal Vision[1]

In order for you to use an Ideal Vision and get the most power from it, here are some guidelines:

1. An Ideal Vision is ideal. It defines, in measurable perform-ance terms, the kind of world you and your partners want to create together for tomorrow's child.

2. Take the long view; don't be constricted by the here-and-now.

3. Dream. Be idealistic. Imagine a perfect world.[2]

4. Don't worry if, at first, it doesn't seem achievable. You might not be able to get there in your lifetime or your chil-dren's lifetime, but at least you will know where you are headed. You can track your continuous progress: If you are not headed in that direction, what do you have in mind?

5. You and your organization will not be responsible for achieving all of the Ideal Vision, just a part of it.

6. Define ends to be accomplished, not means (or resources). Make the ends, or objectives, measurable on an interval or ratio scale—**measurable** indicators of the kind of world you want for your children and grandchildren.

7. In writing objectives, including the Ideal Vision, use the Mager-type objectives, which state where you are headed and the criteria to be used to track your progress and success.

For each element in the Ideal Vision, build a matrix with each element listed. Then, using Figure 9.1, make sure that at least one of those is used in your strategic, tactical, and operational planning. Doing this will give you a reality check to make sure you are think-ing and planning Mega.

Figure 9.1: Checklist for Ideal Vision

Element of the Ideal Vision	Included in Organizational Purpose
There will be no loss of life nor elimination or reduction of levels of survival, self-sufficiency, or quality of life from any source, including those that follow:	
War, riot, terrorism, or unlawful civil unrest	
Murder, rape, or crimes of violence, robbery, or destruction to property	
Substance abuse	
Shelter	
Permanent or continuing disabilities	
Disease	
Starvation and/or malnutrition	
Destructive behavior (including child, partners, spouse, self, elder, others)	
Accidents, including transportation, home, and business/workplace	
Discrimination, based on irrelevant variables including color, race, age, creed, gender, religion, wealth, national origin, or location	

Is It Reasonable to Think We Can Get the Ideal Vision Accomplished by Me, My Organization, and Now?

While achieving an Ideal Vision should be our intention, it is not likely given the culture and personal concerns of people populating our world, our organizations, and our neighborhoods. The key, then, is in continual improvement as we move relentlessly toward Mega. Each person in the organization—each functional unit in the organization—and the organization itself must move to achieve Mega—to add measurable value to all stakeholders, including themselves.

In operational reality, each organization may set en-route missions as they move for the current What Is in terms of results and value added to internal and external stakeholders to What Should Be. It is useful to develop a **chain of missions** that give benchmarks for everyone as they move from where they are to where they should be. Figure 9.2 includes a hierarchy of missions, or strategic objectives—each one adding to the next more distant one. All lower-level missions cascade down from the Ideal Vision (Mega). Each mission level defines, in measurable terms, what has to be accomplished and delivered on or before the time listed for each.

A key to making such useful and practical decisions is to not be limited to each organizational level as specified, but to constantly strive to see how close you can come to Mega. Continual improvement at each level will have you continually moving closer to Mega—to the Ideal Vision. It is important to keep in mind that objectives state the minimum, not the maximum: You may exceed an objective.

Figure 9.2: A hierarchy of missions.

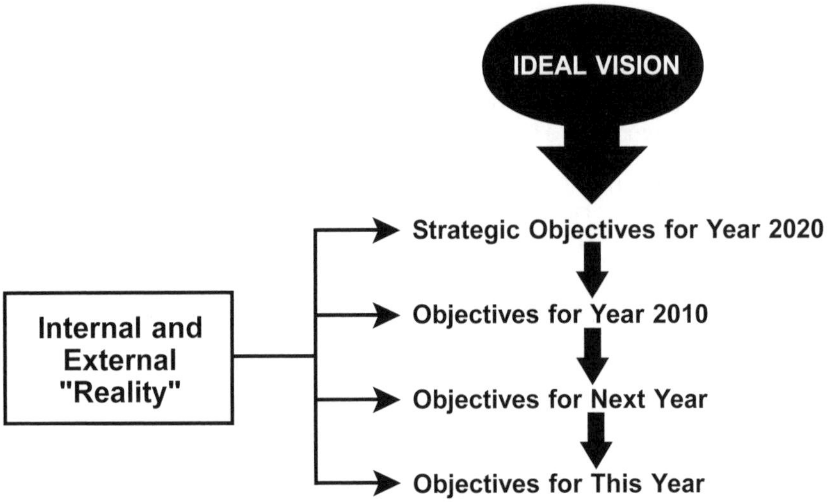

Linking and Aligning Your Progress

As you plan down from Mega, there is a linking and overlap between your objectives and plans as you link and align Mega with Macro with Micro and then with Processes and Inputs, as shown in Figure 9.3. Note the overlap from one function to the next. Each lower level builds on the data generated in the level above: a bridge between levels.

Figure 9.3: The overlap and flow of moving from Mega to Macro to Micro to Processes to Inputs.

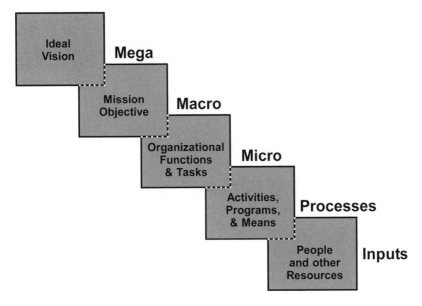

Simultaneity of Planning and Doing:
The Three Levels of Planning (Mega, Macro, Micro)
and Their Relation to Processes and Inputs

Ensuring alignment was first suggested in Figure 3.3. In Figure 9.4 is an application of that important function. Obtaining alignment can be vital for organizational success in order to ensure that programs, projects, policies, and activities usually complement each other. In Figure 9.4, the sequence of events and functions are noted with numbers (1) through (14) to show the order in which a new potential initiative (toaster production training) may be sorted into the Organizational Elements Model and aligned with Policies and

Procedures (Column 3) as well as Laws, Rules, and Regulations (Column 4). Follow the numbers to see the hypothetical flow; successful transfer of skills, knowledge, attitudes, and abilities (SKAAS) should add value to that product as it moves from within the organization to a consumer. By placing it, toaster production training, in the alignment table, you may observe what is possibly missing and what has to be accomplished in order to ensure linkage and to make sure that what you use, do, produce, and deliver will add value both within the organization and outside of it.

Figure 9.4: Alignment table used for a potential product.

Organizational Elements Model	Program, Project, Activity	Policies, Procedures	Laws, Rules, Regulations
Mega	(13) Customer satisfaction met as well as documented zero losses of life, permanent disabilities, or reduction of customer well-being from delivered toasters. Additionally, product line approved by Underwriters Labs for safety.	(14) All products (including the toaster)must have complete safety and have no successful lawsuits or government restrictions or sanctions on any product. Performance data must substantiate these requirements.	(3) Any product must be safe for the purpose intended and meet safety standards.
Macro	(12) Toasters, packaging, instructions, and warranty materials shipped to customers.	(4) Any suggested training program has to be approved by the production manager and program manager.	

(Continued)

Figure 9.4 (Concluded)

Micro	(5) Managers approve training program based on needs and value added.	(10) Toaster production quality must be tested and certified. (11) Toasters are packed and ready for delivery.	
Process	(1) Training rec-ommendation for toaster production. (7) Performance improvement experiences (train-ing) designed, developed, and formatively evalu-ated. (8) Competent toaster production personnel certified. (9) Toaster produc-tion implemented.		
Input	(6) Existing SKAAs for potential train-ees identified. Operational envi-ronment, including workplace require-ments, identified and approved.	(2) Training must be based on a needs assessment and produce meas-urable SKAAs that add internal and external value.	

Moving from Mega to Success

Figure 9.5 lists the steps for performing a Mega-level needs assessment and a management "score card" for scheduling and tracking progress:

Figure 9.5: Steps in conducting a Mega-level needs assessment.

	Person or Group Responsible	Date Assigned	Date Completed
Determine Needs—gaps in results for each component (or "family of components" in the Ideal Vision).			
Prioritize the Needs on the basis of the costs to meet the needs as compared to the costs to ignore them (these might be course-grained estimates).			
Determine your organization's current impact on external clients and society in terms of survival, self-sufficiency, and quality of life.			
Determine the component(s) of the Ideal Vision your organization is committed to deliver and moving ever closer toward, including indicators of its impact on the survival, self-sufficiency, and quality of life of its external clients and our shared society.			
Place Mega-level Needs (gaps in results) between the Ideal Vision and the current status, in priority order, based on the cost to successfully address the problem vs. the cost to ignore the problem.			
Develop an Ideal Vision–linked Mission Objective that includes specific criteria for each gap you choose to address (e.g., what you will have accomplished five, ten, or more years from now).			

(Continued)

Figure 9.5 (Concluded)

Break down your Mission Objective to functional building-block objectives—into functions.			
Obtain formal approval and concurrence of your Macro-level Needs from your clients as well as your internal partners (clients are included throughout the entire process).			
List alternative methods and means for addressing your Mega-level Need(s) and identify the advantages and disadvantages of each: costs and consequences.			

The same rationale is used for doing a needs assessment for each level of planning and results (see Figure 9.6).

Figure 9.6: Steps in conducting a Macro-level
needs assessment.

	Person or Group Responsible	Date Assigned	Date Completed
Specify the desired quality—useful contributions—of what your organization delivers to external clients. *(Remember, starting here assumes—or actually builds on the Mega-level needs assessment— that you have linked to the Ideal Vision level.)*			
Determine the performance requirements in terms of what your organization delivers, in measurable performance terms, to external clients.			
List the identified and agreed-upon need(s).			
Align the needs identified at the Macro-level with the Ideal Vision and mission of your organization.			
Place Macro-level Needs in a priority order, based on the cost to ignore versus the cost to meet each identified need.			
Obtain concurrence of the Macro-level Needs from your internal and external clients.			
List alternative methods and means for addressing your Macro-level Need(s), and identify the advantages and disadvantages of each.			

The same thinking and process holds as you move down to Micro-level needs assessments (see Figure 9.7).

Figure 9.7: Steps in conducting a Micro-level needs assessment.

	Person or Group Responsible	Date Assigned	Date Completed
Determine individuals' and/or small groups' required performance in measurable terms. *(Note that starting at this level assumes linkages to the Macro and Mega levels or that you actually have the identified needs from these two levels.)*			
Determine individuals' and/or small groups' current performance status relative to the required performance standards established in the first step.			
List the identified, agreed-upon Micro-level Need(s).			
Align the needs identified at the Micro-level with the Ideal Vision (Mega) and mission (Macro) of your organization.			
Place Micro-level Needs in a priority order, based on the cost to ignore versus the cost to meet the identified Needs.			
Present your Micro-level Needs to your clients and obtain concurrence.			
List alternative methods and means for addressing your Micro-level Need(s) and identify the advantages and disadvantages of each.			

Collecting and Displaying Needs Assessment Data

Figure 9.8 provides a useful way of summarizing and presenting needs assessment data. Note that, as suggested throughout, you ensure that there is always alignment among Mega, Macro, and Micro.

Figure 9.8: Needs assessment summary format.

	Current Results	Possible Means	Required Results	Related Ideal Vision Element	Need Level Focus		
					Mega	Macro	Micro
1. Collect the needs (gaps in results) data, and enter it into the Needs Assessment Summary Format. Then for each, confirm that:							
a. Each stated need identifies a need as a gap in results;							
b. For each process or resources-referenced statement (that some people might at first mislabel as a "need"), ask, "If we were successful at this, what result would result?" Thus, convert any quasi-need (a gap in methods or a gap in resources) into a need.							

2. For each need identified, classify it as:

- Mega-related
- Macro-related
- Micro-related

Are there needs for Mega, Macro, and Micro? Are they linked and aligned? If not, collect more data to ensure linkage.

3. List the needs and obtain approval of your planning partners.

Using the What Is and What Should Be Format for Collecting Data

An advantage of using *need* only as a noun is that you can use the What Is and What Should Be format to collect useful data and define gaps in results all at the same time. Figure 9.9 is an example.

Figure 9.9: What Is and What Should Be format.

KEY

SA = Strongly Agree   D = Disagree
A = Agree   SD = Strongly Disagree
N = Neutral

| WHAT IS | | | | | Statement (Results-Related)* | WHAT SHOULD BE | | | | |
SA	A	N	D	SD		SA	A	N	D	SD
					1. This organization is client centered.					
					2. Our performance objectives are written in measurable performance terms.					
					3. We plan to deliver value at the Mega level.					
					4. Results, not politics, are rewarded here.					
					5. Evaluation is conducted at the three levels of results: Mega, Macro, and Micro.					
					6. Minority employment policies are attracting and keeping competent people.					
					7. We learn from our mistakes.					
					8. Personnel/HRD policies encourage individual productivity.					

(Continued)

Figure 9.9 (Concluded)

WHAT IS					Statement	WHAT SHOULD BE				
SA	A	N	D	SD	(Results-Related)*	SA	A	N	D	SD
					9. Resources are available when required.					
					10. Resources are of proper quality.					
					11. Deliveries are on time.					
					12. All deliveries meet customer requirements.					
					13. There are zero customer complaints.					
					14. Associates are 100% competent in all skills, knowledge, attitudes, and abilities.					
					15. There are no deaths or disabilities from what we deliver.					
					16. Our workplace is completely safe.					
					17. There are no negative environmental impacts from our work and activities.					
					18. Everyone understands the mission of our organization.					
					19. All associates make a contribution to their work assignment, the organization's Outputs, external clients' success, and societal well-being.					
					20. Etc.					

*Mixed Mega, Macro, and Micro results

This format—based on a needs assessment approach—is very useful for collecting data and ensuring that the data collected identify gaps between current results and desired results. Because this type of data collection is soft or observational data, it is strongly urged that such be compared to hard performance data.

Many so-called needs assessment models exist. Not all really deal with needs. The question any adopter should ask is "How many of the organizational elements are vital to my success?" A comparison of various popular models of so-called and actual needs assessments may be found in:

- Leigh, D., Watkins, R., Platt, W., & Kaufman, R. (2000). Alternate models of needs assessment: Selecting the right one for your organization. *Human Resource Development Quarterly, 11*(1), 87–93.

- Watkins, R., Leigh, D., Platt, W., & Kaufman, R. (1998). Needs assessment: A digest, review, and comparison of needs assessment literature. *Performance Improvement, 37*(7), 40–53.

- Watkins, R., Leigh, D., & Kaufman, R. (1999). Choosing a needs assessment model. In Silberman, M. *Team and Organizational Development Sourcebook.* New York: McGraw-Hill.

How do needs assessments you have used or know about stack up with the requirements for delivering useful data? The exercise in Figure 9.10 could be useful when you are considering a needs assessment you have been involved in or you are looking at that has been used before.

Figure 9.10: Assessing needs assessments.

Using a needs assessment you have developed or recall being used:

1. Compare your needs assessment and determine if it includes:

    1a. _____ Mega-level data

    1b. _____ Macro-level data

    1c. _____ Micro-level data

    (It might be that it is "none of the above.")

    Note: *A way to determine if it is Mega (societal) focused is to determine if elements of an Ideal Vision (Figure 1.1) are included.*

_____ 2. Does your needs assessment focus on ends or means?

_____ 3. What are the implications for your internal (organizational) and external clients' success that will be delivered by the needs assessment you are comparing relative with this (Mega) approach and this exercise?

_____ 4. Does your needs assessment utilize a combination of "hard" and "soft" data collected from a variety of data sources throughout the organization?

Follow-on questions:

5. If the needs assessment does not include a Mega-level focus or links, what will it take to modify it?

6. What are the penalties and payoffs for you and your internal and external clients for using a Mega-level–linked needs assessment? For not using a Mega-level–linked needs assessment?

7. Why do you think most needs assessment models and frameworks don't include or link to the Mega level?

Moving from Mega to Macro to Micro to Processes to Inputs: Solving Problems

It is not enough to identify and prioritize needs, nor is it enough to just identify the requirements for success—for change. While not the topic of this book, Figure 9.11 illustrates the functions, or steps, required to get from "here" to "there"—to deliver success.[3]

Figure 9.11: Steps to delivering success.

1.0 Problem defined on Mega-level needs	2.0 Desired results stated in measurable terms	3.0 Consensus and support built
4.0 Possible causes identified	5.0 Solutions selected and designed	6.0 The means and methods of change selected
7.0 Agreed on course of action (i.e., a plan)	8.0 Constraints and restraints resolved	9.0 Plans, programs, and interventions scheduled
10.0 Implemented and completed	11.0 Impacts and consequences determined	12.0 Revisions and adjustments accomplished

Mega thinking and planning is about defining a shared success, achieving it, and being able to prove it. Mega thinking and planning is a focus not on one's organization alone, but on society now and in the future. It is about adding measurable value to all stakeholders.

Mega thinking and planning has been offered and evolving for many years, perhaps first formally with Kaufman's 1972 *Educational System Planning* and further developed in Kaufman and English, 1979, and continuing through now. In one form or another, using a societal frame for planning and doing has shown up in the works of respected thinkers, including Senge (1990) and more recently

Prahalad (2005) and Davis (2005). For some reason, there continues to be some resistance to Mega thinking and planning—a resistance that seems to be increasingly evaporating as witnessed by the articles in a special issue of *Performance Improvement Quarterly* and indeed other professional contributions around the world. I recommend the continuation of this migration from individual performance as the preferred unit of analysis for performance improvement to one that includes a first consideration of society and external stakeholders. It is responsible, responsive, and ethical to add value to all.

Using the Conceptual Map as a Guide for Mega Thinking and Planning

This framework (shown in Figure 9.12) relates the functions for strategic thinking and planning—from the Ideal Vision through design,[4] development, implementation, and evaluation/continual improvement. In addition, it shows how each phase of the strategic thinking and planning cycle relates to the Six-Step Problem-Solving Process (Figure 3.7).

You can check your thinking and doing against this framework and see where you are in the process and double-check to make certain you are using all of the elements of strategic planning.

Figure 9.12: A Relationship Map of Mega Thinking, Planning, and Doing: Relating Tools and Concepts[5]

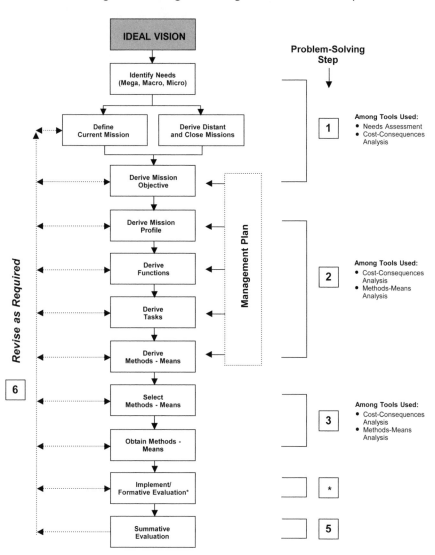

*This is also part of Step 6; revise as required.

Endnotes

1. Based on Kaufman (1998).

2. In earlier works, I called using an Ideal Vision "practical dreaming."

3. Based on Kaufman (2000).

4. First developed by Ingrid Guerra, Wayne State University.

5. Some of the terms used here are to be found in other works, such as Kaufman, 2000. *Methods-Means analysis* is the tool for identifying alternative ways and means to meet needs and identifies the advantages and disadvantages of each. *Costs-consequences analysis* estimates the costs of accomplishing something as compared to the costs of doing nothing. It can also look at the benefits as related to meeting needs for alternative means and methods.

Chapter 10
Applications: Putting Strategic
Thinking and Planning to Work

It is now time to apply the concepts, models, processes, and tools provided in Chapters 1 through 9. Rather than have you go back and search each time, critical figures will be repeated here, in the context of applications.

Although there are lots of strategic planning models and processes available, most are incomplete, but they are popular. It will be to your advantage to heed the advice of Critical Success Factor 1: Don't assume that what has worked for you and others in the past will work for you now.

Review of Models

When defining where to head and justifying why you want to go there, use some of the basics provided earlier, including:

1. The Three Cs:
   Change
   Choice
   Consequences

2. The Ideal Vision: Mega—where to head

3. The Six Critical Success Factors: making sure you get to where you should go

4. The Six-Step Problem-Solving Process: finding and implementing the best ways and means to get from here to there

Know What Not to Do as Well as What to Do

In addition to knowing the right things to use and do, you can also benefit from knowing what *not* to do—choosing what is useful, not simply what is conventional. We can count on change happening; we can take control or wait for things to happen to us. We may be proactive or reactive. Be proactive.

Business Plans and Mega Planning

In most organizational activities, one is expected to provide a "business plan." Business plans, at their best, identify and document the relationship between what is spent (time, money, resources) and what benefits are derived for the organization in the short run. Business plans usually stop at Macro—the payoffs for the organization—and usually relate to payoffs in immediate fiscal quarters or immediate years.

As sensible as this might seem at first, conventional business plans almost always fail to formally factor in the value added to external clients and society. Because they do not include Mega, they are incomplete. It is risky to base any plan, including a business plan, only on return on investment/return on equity for the organization alone.

We urge that a "business plan plus" be used that includes all of the elements of a conventional business plan as well as linking all of that to measurable value added for the organization, external clients, and our shared society.

Avoiding the Conventional Wisdom and the Conventional Traps in Strategic Planning— Not Making the Usual Mistakes

Most people would like to improve the chances of arriving alive and successful in the future. Interestingly, what is *usually* done is at best not strategic, and at worst destructive. Here is a guide to avoiding the general approaches, tools, and concepts that don't work.

Conventional Strategic Planning Mistake #1: Call All Levels of Planning "Strategic." While not aligning Societal value added, organizational contributions and the value added from that, and individual performance contributions and that value added.

Given the popularity of strategic planning, in order to be in vogue, people call any kind of planning "strategic"; that turns out to not be rational, realistic, or functional. In reality (and sensible practice), there are actually three levels of planning: strategic, tactical, and operational. These three levels account for and align what any organization uses, does, produces, and delivers that add measurable value to external clients (see Figure 10.1).

Figure 10.1: Levels of planning table—A review.

Type of Planning (and its level of Planning/Major Focus)	Identifies External Value Added; Can Add New Organizational Purposes and Delete Existing Ones	Identifies Possible Ways and Means to Meet the Strategic Objectives in Order to Select the Most Effective and Efficient	Makes Sure the Selected Tactics and Tools Work Properly
Strategic (Mega level)	✓		
Tactical (Macro level)		✓	
Operational (Micro level)			✓

Conventional Strategic Planning Mistake #2: Use a "Systems" Approach

As commonly used (and abused), a *systems* perspective focuses on one area out of the whole, such as Human Performance Technology (HPT), workplace learning, marketing, selling, manufacturing, or organizational culture. It calls notice to how any area of attention (usually and inappropriately called "the system") is complex and then intends to look at all of the interactions among those immediate parts of the "hunk" they have targeted—thus a *systems perspective*. A systems approach looks only at pieces, parts, isolated elements and never looks at any organization as a whole that is nested in our shared society.

The basic, ethical, practical, and most useful *system approach* for any strategic thinking and planning takes as its primary perspective society, now and in the future. This level of planning is called the *Mega level,* where the primary client and beneficiary is society. If you are not adding value to society, you are likely subtracting value.[1]

Conventional Strategic Planning Mistake #3: Confuse Ends and Means and Blur Strategy, Tactics, Operations, and Methods

Many people think *strategy* is about means or "how-to-do-its." That isn't helpful. Strategy is about ends, consequences, and results. Strategic planning doesn't talk about means, resources, methods, or techniques. It only defines and justifies what value we are to add to external clients and society. Tactical planning is based on strategic planning results and identifies possible ways and means to meet strategic (Mega) objectives. Operations are about using what you selected (based on previous plans) and applying appropriate methods. Strategic, tactical, and operational planning is about defining and specifying useful ends.

Conventional Strategic Planning Mistake #4: Prepare Objectives that Include the Methods and Resources in the Statement

Objectives should never include *how* you are going to get the result accomplished.[2] To do so is just plain destructive; it is selecting the solution before you have defined and justified the problem—a confusing of ends and means.

Conventional Strategic Planning Mistake #5: Base Your Strategic Plan Only on Perceptions, Not on Performance-Results Data

If the strategic plan is not based on delivering required results and payoffs, it won't be useful. And just getting people's perceptions about means, methods, tools, and techniques without formally linking those means to actual performance results will likely deliver a weak or useless strategic plan.

How does one get the valid performance data on which to base a useful plan? Not by just asking people. One gets it by doing a "needs assessment" (not a "wants assessment") where gaps in results for external clients and society are identified and selected. Then, both the hard data (actual performance) and soft data (perceptions) can be compared and integrated.

Conventional Strategic Planning Mistake #6: Assume that There are Just Some Things That Are Not Measurable

The truth is, contrary to conventional (and uninformed) wisdom, if you can name it, you are measuring it. There are mathematical scales of measurement for purposes that are stated in nominal, ordinal, interval, and ratio scales. A problem doesn't cease to exist simply by ignoring it. Get indicators for everything you intend to do and accomplish, even if putting them in nominal or ordinal scale terms is the best you can do.

Conventional Strategic Planning Mistake #7: Define *Needs* as Gaps in Resources or Methods (and thus confusing Ends and Means)

Unfortunate for performance accomplishment professionals is the day that Maslow and his "Hierarchy of Needs" became the Holy Grail of performance improvement. If you want to follow this fine gentleman's advice and use *need* as a verb—a means or a resource—you will have good but failing company.

If you want to avoid the sin of not basing your strategic plan on hard performance data, never use *need* as a verb; use it only to define a gap in results. Any time you use *need* as a verb—such as "need to," "need for," "needing"—you are moving to select means and resources before defining and substantiating a problem as a gap in results that should be closed.

Conventional Strategic Planning Mistake #8: Do a "Training Needs Assessment"

A "training needs assessment" usually places focus on a means—training—and not ends—performance. If you believe Deming and Juran, starting with training—a means focused on individual performance improvement, not an end such as competent performance—you will be wrong 80 to 90 percent of the time. Why? They note that 80 to 90 percent of all performance breakdowns are not individual performance breakdowns, but system (and I suggest also external) breakdowns. Why do one before doing a needs assessment at the Mega, Macro, and Micro levels? No matter how well you fix a performance problem at the individual performance level, if the real problem is elsewhere, all you do is spend money and frustrate people.

Conventional Strategic Planning Mistake #9: Let a Friendly Group Develop the Strategic Plan

Any plan, any initiative, any change (and strategic plans, by their nature, usually call for change) will predictably fail if people who are charged with implementing it feel they were not part of its development. So, even though it is a bit more challenging, get a representative group of stakeholders to develop the plan. To obtain what Peter Drucker terms *transfer of ownership,* be sure that both internal and external clients as well as society are represented. In addition, when you only use friends to develop a plan, they will tend to look after themselves and please their bosses and might shy away from real needs, real problems, and real opportunities.

Conventional Strategic Planning Mistake #10: Target Your Organization as the Primary Beneficiary of the Strategic Plan

If strategic planning stops at your organization's front door, you might be on your way to becoming another Enron, WorldCom, Tyco, or Andersen. They all took themselves on (and a few executives took themselves on as the most important beneficiaries) as the basic client of the strategic plan. And if you really like failed strategic plans, go and benchmark theirs. You are what you do and accomplish, not simply what you say.

Conventional Strategic Planning Mistake #11: Dismiss All of This as "Not Practical, Not Real World," or "Because This is Not What the 'Big' People Do"

You are right. What is suggested here is not the conventional wisdom. And it is not the way Enron, Tyco, Andersen, or the dot.coms did strategic planning. It is also not the way most people know, think about, and do what they call strategic thinking.

If you want to avoid disastrous mistakes, following is a review of the six critical success factors for doing strategic planning that will help you define the future and deliver it. It is a view from higher altitude than common that will point you in the right direction. Is it magic? No. But it combines practicality and ethics. It could well put an end to conventional mistakes when attempting strategic planning that fails.

Six Critical Success Factors of
Strategic Thinking and Planning—A Review[3]

1. Don't assume that what worked in the past will work now. Get out of your comfort zone and be open to change.
2. Differentiate between ends (what) and means (how).
3. Use and link all three levels of planning and results: Mega/Outcomes, Macro/Outputs, and Micro/Products.
4. Prepare all objectives (including those for Mega, Macro, and Micro levels) that rigorously state where you are headed and how to tell when you have arrived.
5. Define *need* as a gap between current and desired results, not as insufficient levels of means or resources.
6. Use an Ideal Vision (the kind of world we want to create for tomorrow's child stated in measurable terms) as the basis for all thinking and planning: the Mega level.

Another template is the Organizational Elements Model. This model will ensure that you link all ends and means and that you integrate strategic, tactical, and operational planning.

Name of the Organizational Element	Brief Description and Level of Focus	Type of Planning
Mega	Results and their consequences for external clients and society (shared vision)	Strategic
Macro	The results and their consequences for what an organization can or does deliver outside of itself	Tactical
Micro	The results and their consequences for individuals and small groups within the organization	Operational
Process	Means, programs, projects, activities, methods, techniques	
Input	Human, capital, and physical resources; existing rules, regulations, policies, laws	

And finally, the Six-Step Problem-Solving Process will allow you to perform the functions to get you from What Is to What Should Be.

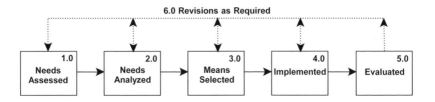

Using these tools and concepts, you can choose to avoid the 11 conventional mistakes that can derail any strategic planning effort. A decision checklist is provided in Figure 10.2.

Figure 10.2: Avoiding making conventional mistakes
when doing strategic thinking and planning.

Possible Conventional Mistakes to Do When Doing Strategic Planning	Currently Do	Will Continue to Do	Will Change What I Do
1. Call all levels of planning "strategic."*			
2. Use a "system̲s" approach.			
3. Confuse ends and means and blur strategy, tactics, operations, and methods.			
4. Prepare objectives that include the methods and resources in the statement.			
5. Base your strategic plan only on perceptions, not on performance-results data.			
6. Assume that there are just some things that are not measurable.			
7. Define *needs* as gaps in resources or methods (and thus confusing ends and means).			
8. Do a "training needs assessment."			
9. Let a friendly group develop the strategic plan.			
10. Target your organization as the primary beneficiary of the strategic plan.			
11. Dismiss all of this as "not practical, not real world," or "because this is not what the 'big' people do."			

*(While not aligning societal value added, organizational contributions and value added, and individual performance contributions and value added value.)

To further guide you in strategic planning and thinking, here is a checklist to help you.

A Strategic Planner's Checklist

☐   1.   Remember that one of the most painful things you can ask anyone (including yourself) to endure is change.

☐   2.   Be gentle, objective, and caring. Share the possibilities and positive consequences that can and will evolve. Don't be a bully. Never accuse. Never abuse. Listen. Consider what people tell you. Take the approach of "come let us reason together."

☐   3.   Get people away from the security of their offices and the built-in, run-and-hide excuses of being too busy to plan, answering their desk or cell phones, responding to memos, having to crank out that overdue report, putting out "fires." Go to a neutral area and break the ice before getting down to the realities of proactive planning. Model and build trust.

☐   4.   Realize that proactive planning often carries an implied (even if unintended) criticism of the current approach, processes, regime, conventions, and culture. State that possibility very early, and get it on the table.

☐   5.   Bring to everyone's attention that proactive strategic thinking and planning is *their* tool—their opportunity to make the kind of contribution, individually and together, they really want to deliver. Show them how they, by using proactive planning, can be in control and be the masters of change, not its victims.

☐   6.   Ask, don't tell. Don't be accusatory in your questions. Such phrases as "Isn't it possible that..." or "I feel..." often reduce the possibility of sending an unspoken, unwitting accusatory message.

7. Be clear. Use the language of the group, but don't change meanings only in order to have them accept you. Often people use words that are fuzzy or have too many alternative meanings. Don't water down the precision of your words and message or continually shift your meanings to fit with current biases; doing so risks falling into the "We already do that" trap. Be precise, be comfortable, maintain rigor. Get common working definitions.

8. Be patient. When people react, get defensive, start assigning blame, or attack you, recognize and acknowledge their frustration. And realize that you might get out of your comfort zone and deal with that possibility.

9. Don't affix blame on others. Steer clear of the "we/they" divisions. Help all to envision new contributions, to set fresh horizons, and to reaffirm current useful purposes.

10. Don't take it personally when you, the "messenger," are attacked. If you have followed the above guidelines, if you are without hidden agendas, and if you really do care about the people, organization, and community, you are there to help, and the right results and approach will evolve. Don't forget that some people get afraid if what they are currently doing and thinking are subjected to rational alternatives.

11. Don't deviate from Mega—adding value to external clients and society—even if pressed and pushed. Mega is the practical and ethical destination.

12. Model and use the Six Critical Success Factors, the Organizational Elements Model (OEM), and the Six-Step Problem-Solving Process.

13. Find a sponsor, or champion, for strategic thinking and planning: the higher up in the organization and the greater their credibility, the better.

Selecting Who Should Be on the Strategic Planning Team

Deciding who actually does the strategic planning (everyone should do strategic thinking) is vital. Here are some guidelines[4] to follow when deciding who the planning team should include:

1. Level of position, power, and authority—those who represent the internal and external partners

2. Level of strategic thinking and planning skills and competencies—all should think, act, and plan Mega

3. Level of commitment to the organization—don't include those who are just "serving time"

4. Level of technical expertise relevant to the core capabilities of the organization; they should know their jobs, know the jobs of others, perform magnificently, and know how all the jobs should go together to deliver success

5. Level of authentic leadership skills and competencies

6. Open, honest, and sincere with no hidden objectives or single-issue agendas

14 Basic Steps for Defining and Delivering Success: Mega Planning[5]

Figure 10.3 illustrates 14 steps for thinking, doing, and delivering Mega results and consequences.

Figure 10.3: 14 steps to Mega planning.

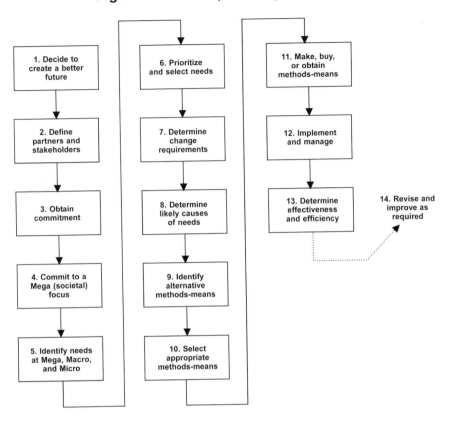

Look at each step shown in Figure 10.3 briefly:

Planning

1. **Decide to create a better future.** Mega thinking and planning is about improving our shared world using yourselves and your organizations as the vehicle. This proactive approach—based on helping to create the kind of world we want for tomorrow's child—is the single most important feature and is the primary "active ingredient" of this approach.

2. **Define partners and stakeholders.** Strategic thinking and planning should not be a lonely endeavor. If Mega planning is to add measurable value to our shared world, its development and implementation must be shared as well; shared with the

people who will be impacted by it and the people who will implement it. Without "transfer of ownership,"[6] any plans and resulting programs and activities will be at jeopardy.

Not only does everyone who will implement and receive the consequences of Mega planning have to "buy in" to its creations and its results, there must be sponsors for the planning activities and resulting plans. The higher up in the organization you can get sponsors, the better. The sponsor(s) should be in key decision-making roles and seen by all to have credibility and the ability to support the plans once developed.[7]

Sponsors, supporters, and participants should represent those who can and will be impacted by changes or failures to change. Don't select people simply because they are friends or politically connected. Everyone should know that Mega planning is bias-free.

3 & 4. **Get commitment.** No lip-service or passive support are allowed. Get all the players to actually sign off. The strategic thinking and planning agreement table (Figure 4.4) can get you started to make sure that all involved partners agree on Mega and the linkages among levels of results and consequences.

5. **Identify needs at the Mega, Macro, and Micro levels.** Because organizations must link external client and societal contributions (Mega) with organizational contributions (Macro) and individual and small group contributions (Micro), needs—gaps in results—at each level must be harvested.

Needs at the Mega level should be based on the Ideal Vision (Figure 1.1), and these gaps in results will serve to provide you with the mission objective. The mission objective is the measurable statement of what your organization will deliver to move it ever closer to the needs identified in the Ideal Vision. Figure 9.3 shows how the various levels are linked and related as you move from Mega to Macro to Micro.

6. **Prioritize and select needs.** Because needs are gaps in results, prioritization should be done on the basis of costs-consequences assessment—the costs to meet the needs as compared to the costs for ignoring them. Needs should be prioritized at the Mega, Macro, and Micro levels. Guides for prioritizing and selecting needs are provided in Chapter 8.

7. **Determine change requirements.** This step asks that you compare your current results and methods-means with the required ones so that you may identify what should be changed in your organization (results, resources, methods, etc.) and what you should keep and maintain. The priorities derived in Step 6 provide the criteria.

8. **Determine likely causes of the needs.** Now that you have identified the changes and what should be continued, you can do an analysis of what is causing the gaps in results for the needs you want to reduce or eliminate. For example, current levees might contain the ravages of a category 3 storm and you want them to resist a category 4 storm. What are the causes of current failures? Politics, fraud, engineering, funding, commitment, cooperation, maintenance? This is where you find the reasons for the current priority gaps so that you can identify what must change.

9. **Identify alternative methods and means.** Now you survey all of the possible ways and means to close the gaps in results—needs—you have selected and list the advantages and disadvantages of each. For example, one method-mean would be government funding of levee reconstruction. An advantage would be in the immediacy of funds. A possible disadvantage could be that any funding would be wasted.

Doing

10. **Select the appropriate methods and means.** This is getting into the implementation of the strategic/Mega plan. Based on costs-consequences (what you get and what you give), you pick the most effective and efficient ways and resources to meet the needs.

11. **Make or buy or obtain the methods and means.** This is more of implementation. As the athletic footwear ads note, "Just do it." There are many performance design, development, and implementation approaches available for this. Several recommended ones are in the balance of this series of books.

12. **Implement and manage.** Against the performance criteria developed earlier, ensure that everything stays on course and on schedule, and meets all requirements. If not developing appropriately, revise as required.

13. **Determine effectiveness and efficiency.** This is summative evaluation. You compare your results with your objectives and identify what worked and what did not, all based on measurable criteria and performance.

14. **Revise as required.** Each short-fall is a friend in disguise for it tells you what must be changed to deliver success. Evaluation (#13 above) should never be for blaming, but rather for fixing, and here is where the fixing can happen. Change what should be changed and keep what is working. This step is actually done both at this stage of planning and doing as well as at each of the previous steps.

Getting Help and Guidance that Are Available

This book doesn't provide everything you might use—just the basics for strategic thinking and planning. For example, concepts and tools for systems analysis (Step 2 in the Six-Step Problem-Solving Process, Figure 3.7) and planning tools such as flowcharting are available elsewhere. Also, the methods and concepts for performance system design, development, and implementation are available elsewhere (including the balance of the five books in this series), although all should be linked to the overall system direction and requirements (the subject of this book).

My other books that deal with the concepts and tools presented in this book would be useful, especially:

Kaufman, R. (1998). *Strategic thinking: A guide to identifying and solving problems (Revised)*. Washington, D.C. & Arlington, VA: The International Society for Performance Improvement and the American Society for Training and Development. (Recipient of the 2001 International Society for Performance Improvement "Outstanding Instructional Communication Award.") Also, Spanish edition, *El Pensamiento Estrategico*. Centro de Estudios: Roman Areces, S.A., Madrid, Spain.

Kaufman, R. (2000). *Mega planning: Practical tools for organizational success.* Thousand Oaks, CA: Sage Publications. Also *Planificación Mega: Herramientas practices paral el exito organizacional.* (2004). Traducción de Sonia Agut. Universitat Jaume I, Castelló de la Plana, Espana.

Kaufman, R. (2006). *30 seconds that can change your life: A decision-making guide for those who refuse to be mediocre.* Amherst, MA: HRD Press.

Kaufman, R., Guerra, I., and Platt, W. A. (2006). *Practical evaluation for educators: Finding what works and what doesn't.* Thousand Oaks, CA: Corwin Press/Sage.

Kaufman, R., Oakley-Browne, H., Watkins, R., & Leigh, D. (2003). *Strategic planning for success: Aligning people, performance, and payoff.* San Francisco, CA: Jossey-Bass/Pfeiffer.

Useful concepts and tools are also available in other books in this series, including those by Brethower (2006), Gerson (2006), Watkins (2006), Carleton (2006), and Guerra (2006).

The literature that is noted in the References section at the back of this book provides alternatives, methods, means, and actions that might be useful *after* you define where you are headed and justified why you want to get there. Always match your means to the ends you have defined and justified.

When using the fruits of strategic thinking and planning, the functions—building-block results—to be accomplished can be useful if shown in the form of a function-flow block diagram. Such a flowchart shows what building-block results are to be accomplished and the order, or flow, for their accomplishment presented graphically. It is suggested that the formats and procedures for this are beyond the scope of this book. If there is interest (and I hope there is), please review the ways and means for doing this in Kaufman, R. (2000), *Mega Planning.*

To define and deliver measurable success, first apply the concepts and tools in this book. They will help guide you to measurable success—help you define measurable success and be able to prove that success.

To Close and Invite Your Success

These are the basics of strategic thinking and planning. More details on concepts and tools may be found in the References section.

The choice is yours. You know that every personal and organizational life includes the three Cs: Change, Choice, and Consequence.

If you choose to be strategic—if you choose to define and justify where you are headed before you select how to get there—you are best assured that the changes you face and create will be met with sensible choices in order for you and your organization to harvest positive consequences.

We invite those choices.

Endnotes

1. This insight provided by Professor Emeritus Dale Brethower. I wish I had thought of it first, but I didn't.

2. Mager, 1977, is very clear about what an objective should and should not include.

3. Based on Kaufman (1998, 2000).

4. Based in part on Kaufman, Oakley-Browne, Watkins, & Leigh (2003).

5. This 14-step process for achieving high impact—Mega—results was inspired by Kaufman and Stone (1982) and also provided in Kaufman, Oakley-Browne, Watkins, & Leigh (2003).

6. This concept is from Peter Drucker (1973).

7. Some basics on this may be found in Lick, D., & Kaufman, R. (2000–2001: Winter). Change creation: The rest of the planning story. *Planning for Higher Education, 29*(2), 24–36; Roberts, W. (1987). *Leadership secrets of Attila the Hun.* New York: Warner; Conner, D. R. (1992, 2006). *Managing at the speed of change.* New York: Villard Books, Division of Random House; Conner, D. R. (1998). *Building nimble organizations.* New York: John Wiley & Sons, among other sources on change and leadership.

Glossary of Terms[1]

This glossary includes definitions already provided. This is a complete summary of important terms and concepts.

System, systems, systematic, and systemic: related but not the same

system approach: Begins with the sum total of parts working independently and together to achieve a useful set of results at the societal level, adding value for all internal and external partners. We best think of it as the large whole and we can show it thus:

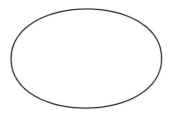

systems approach: Begins with the parts of a system—subsystems—that make up the "system." We can show it thus:

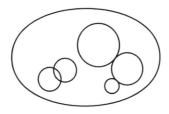

It should be noted here that the "system" is made up of smaller elements, or subsystems, shown as bubbles embedded in the larger system. If we start at this smaller level, we will start with a part and not the whole. So, when someone says they are using a "systems approach" they are really focusing on one or more subsystems, but they are unfortunately focusing on the parts and not the whole. When planning and doing at this level, they can only assume that the payoffs and consequences will add up to something useful to society and external clients, and this is usually a very big assumption.

systematic approach: An approach that does things in an orderly, predictable, and controlled manner. It is a reproducible process. Doing things, however, in a systematic manner does not ensure the achievement of useful results.

systemic approach: An approach that affects everything in the system. The definition of *the system* is usually left up to the practitioner and may or may not include external clients and society. It does not necessarily mean that when something is systemic it is also useful.

Now, let's turn to other strategic thinking and planning terms.

AADDIE model: The ADDIE model with the vital function of Assessment added to the front of it.

ADDIE model: A contraction of the conventional instructional systems steps of Analysis, Design, Development, Implementation, and Evaluation. It ignores or assumes a front determination through assessment of what to analyze, and it also assumes that the evaluation data will be used for continuous improvement.

change creation: The definition and justification, proactively, of new and justified as well as justifiable destinations. If this is done before change management, acceptance is more likely. This is a proactive orientation for change and differs from the more usual *change management* in that it identifies in advance where individuals and organizations are headed rather than waiting for change to occur and be managed.

change management: Ensuring that whatever change is selected will be accepted and implemented successfully by people in the organization. Change management is reactive in that it waits until change requirements are either defined or imposed and then moves to have the change accepted and used.

comfort zones: The psychological areas, in business or in life, where one feels secure and safe (regardless of the reality of that feeling). Change is usually painful for most people. When faced with change, many people will find reasons (usually not rational) for why not to make and modifications. This gives rise to Tom Peter's (1997) observation that "it is easier to kill an organization than it is to change it."

constraints: Anything that will not allow one to meet the results specifications. These might arise from many sources, including not enough resources, insufficient time, political pressures, and the like.

costs-consequences analysis: The process of estimating a return-on-investment analysis before an intervention is implemented. It asks two basic questions simultaneously: what do you expect to give and what do you expect to get back in terms of results? Most formulations do not compute costs and consequences for society and external client (Mega) return on investment. Thus, even the calculations for standard approaches steer away from the vital consideration of self-sufficiency, health, and well-being (Kaufman & Keller [1994]; Kaufman, Keller, & Watkins [1998]; Kaufman [1998, 2000]).

criteria: Precise and rigorous specifications that allow one to prove what has been or has to be accomplished. Many processes in place today do not use rigorous indicators for expected performance. If criteria are "loose" or unclear, there is no realistic basis for evaluation and continuous improvement. Loose criteria often meet the comfort test, but don't allow for the humanistic approach to care enough about others to define, with stakeholders, where you are headed and how to tell when you have or have not arrived.

deep change: Change that extends from Mega—societal value added—downward into the organization to define and shape Macro, Micro, Processes, and Inputs. It is termed *deep change* to note that it is not superficial or just cosmetic, or even a splintered quick fix. Most planning models do not include Mega results in the change process, and thus miss the opportunity to find out what impact their contributions and results have on external clients and society. The other approaches might be termed *superficial change* or *limited change* in that they only focus on an organization or a small part of an organization.

desired results: Ends (or results) identified through needs assessments that are derived from soft data relating to "perceived needs." *Desired* indicates these are perceptual and personal in nature.

ends: Results, achievements, consequences, payoffs, and/or impacts. The more precise the results, the more likely that reasonable methods and means can be considered, implemented, and evaluated. Without rigor for results statements, confusion can take the place of successful performance.

evaluation: Compares current status (what is) with intended status (what was intended) and is most commonly done only after an intervention is implemented. Unfortunately, *evaluation* is used for blaming and not fixing or improving. When blame follows evaluation, people tend to avoid the means and criteria for evaluation or leave them so loose that any result can be explained away.

external needs assessment: Determining and prioritizing gaps, then selecting problems to be resolved at the Mega level. This level of needs assessment is most often missing from conventional approaches. Without the data from it, one cannot be assured that there will be strategic alignment from internal results to external value added.

hard data: Performance data that are based on objectives and independently verifiable. This type of data is critical. It should be used along with "soft" or perception data.

Ideal Vision: The measurable definition of the kind of world we, together with others, commit to help deliver for tomorrow's child. An Ideal Vision defines the Mega level of planning. It allows an organization and all of its partners to define where they are headed and how to tell when they are getting there or getting closer. It provides the rationality and reasons for an organizational mission objective.

Inputs: The ingredients, raw materials, and physical and human resources that an organization can use in its processes in order to deliver useful ends. These ingredients and resources are often the only considerations made during planning without determining the value they add internally and externally to the organization.

internal needs assessment: Determining and prioritizing gaps, then selecting problems to be resolved at the Micro and Macro levels. Most needs assessment processes are of this variety (Watkins, Leigh, Platt, & Kaufman [1998]).

learning: The demonstrated acquisition of a skill, knowledge, attitude, and/or ability.

learning organization: An organization that sets measurable performance standards and constantly compares its results and their consequences with what is required. Learning organizations use performance data, related to an Ideal Vision and the primary mission objective, to decide what to change and what to continue—it learns from its performance and contributions. Learning organizations may obtain the highest level of success by strategic thinking: focusing everything that is used, done, produced, and delivered on Mega results—societal value added. Many conventional definitions do not link the "learning" to societal value added. If there is no external societal linking, then it could well guide one away from the new requirements.

Macro level of planning: Planning focused on the organization itself as the primary client and beneficiary of what is planned and delivered. This is the conventional starting and stopping place for existing planning approaches.

means: Processes, activities, resources, methods, or techniques used to deliver a result. Means are only useful to the extent that they deliver useful results at all three levels of planned results: Mega, Macro, and Micro.

Mega level of planning: Planning focused on external clients, including customers/citizens and the community and society that the organization serves. This is the usual missing planning level in most formulations. It is the only one that will focus on societal value added: survival, self-sufficiency, and quality of life of all partners. It is suggested that this type of planning is imperative for getting and proving useful results. It is this level that Rummler refers to as *primary processes* and Brethower calls the *receiving system.*

Mega thinking: Thinking about every situation, problem, or opportunity in terms of what you use, do, produce, and deliver as having to add value to external clients and society. Same as *strategic thinking.*

methods-means analysis: Identifies possible tactics and tools for meeting the needs identified in a *system analysis.* The methods-means analysis identifies the possible ways and means to meet the needs and achieve the detailed objectives that are identified in this Mega plan, but does not select them. Interestingly, this is a comfortable place where some operational planning starts. Thus, it either assumes or ignores the requirement to measurably add value within and outside the organization.

Micro-level planning: Planning focused on individuals or small groups (such as desired and required competencies of associates or supplier competencies). Planning for building-block results. This also is a comfortable place where some operational planning starts. Starting here usually assumes or ignores the requirement to measurably add value to the entire organization as well as to outside the organization.

mission analysis: Analysis step that identified: (1) what results and consequences are to be achieved; (2) what criteria (in interval and/or ratio scale terms) will be used to determine success; and (3) what are the building-block results and the order of their completion (functions) required to move from the current results to the desired state of affairs. Most mission objectives have not been formally linked to Mega results and consequences, and thus strategic alignment with "where the clients are" are usually missing (Kaufman, Stith, Triner, & Watkins [1998]).

mission objective: An exact, performance-based statement of an organization's overall intended results that it can and should deliver to external clients and society. A mission objective is measurable on an interval or ratio scale, so it states not only "where we are headed" but also adds "how we will know when we have arrived." A mission objective is best linked to Mega levels of planning and the Ideal Vision to ensure societal value added.

mission statement: An organization's Macro-level "general purpose." A mission statement is only measurable on a nominal or ordinal scale of measurement and only states "where we are headed" and leaves rigorous criteria for determining how one measures successful accomplishment.

need: The gap between current results and desired or required results. This is where a lot of planning goes "off the rails." By defining any gap as a *need,* one fails to distinguish between means and ends and thus confuses what and how. If *need* is defined as a gap in results, then there is a triple bonus: (1) it states the objectives (What Should Be), (2) it contains the evaluation and continuous improvement criteria (What Should Be), and (3) it provides the basis for justifying any proposal by using both ends of a need—What Is and What Should Be in terms of results. Proof can be given for the costs to meet the need as well as the costs to ignore the need.

needs analysis: Taking the determined gaps between adjacent organizational elements, and finding the causes of the inability for delivering required results. A needs analysis also identifies possible ways and means to close the gaps in results— needs—but does not select them. Unfortunately, *needs analysis* is usually interchangeable with *needs assessment.* They are not the same. How does one "analyze" something (such as a need) before they know what should be analyzed? First assess the needs, then analyze them.

needs assessment: A formal process that identifies and documents gaps between current and desired and/or required results, arranges them in order of priority on basis of the cost to meet the need as compared to the cost of ignoring it, and selects problems to be resolved. By starting with a needs assessment, justifiable performance data and the gaps between What Is and What Should Be will provide the realistic and rational reason for both what to change as well as what to continue.

objectives: Precise statement of purpose, or destination of where we are headed and how we will be able to tell when we have arrived. The four parts to an objective are (1) what result is to be demonstrated, (2) who or what will demonstrate the results, (3) where will the result be observed, (4) what interval or ratio scale criteria will be used? Loose or process-oriented objectives will confuse everyone (c.f. Mager [1997]). A Mega-level result is best stated as an objective.

outcomes: Results and payoffs at the external client and societal level. Outcomes are results that add value to society, community, and external clients of the organization. These are results at the Mega level of planning.

outputs: The results and payoffs that an organization can or does deliver outside of itself to external clients and society. These are results at the Macro level of planning where the primary client and beneficiary is the organization itself. It does not formally link to outcomes and societal well-being unless it is derived from outcomes and the Ideal (Mega) Vision.

paradigm: The framework and ground rules individuals use to filter reality and understand the world around them (Barker [1992]). It is vital that people have common paradigms that guide them. That is one of the functions of the Mega level of planning and outcomes so that everyone is headed to a common destination and may uniquely contribute to that journey.

performance: A result or consequence of any intervention or activity, including individual, team, or organization: an end.

performance accomplishment system (PAS): Any of a variety of interventions (such as "instructional systems design and development," quality management/continuous improvement, benchmarking, reengineering, and the like) that are results oriented and are intended to get positive results. These are usually focused at the Micro/Products level. This is my preferred alternative to the rather sterile term *performance technology* that often steers people toward hardware and premature solutions (Kaufman [1999, 2000]).

Processes: The means, processes, activities, procedures, interventions, programs, and initiatives an organization can or does use in order to deliver useful ends. While most planners start here, it is dangerous not to derive the Processes and Inputs from what an organization must deliver and the payoffs for external clients.

products: The building-block results and payoffs of individuals and small groups that form the basis of what an organization produces and delivers, inside as well as outside of itself, and the payoffs for external clients and society. Products are results at the Micro level of planning.

quasi-need: A gap in a method, resource, or process. Many so-called "need assessments" are really quasi-needs assessments since they tend to pay immediate attention to means (such as training) before defining and justifying the ends and consequences (Watkins, Leigh, Platt, & Kaufman [1998]).

required results: Ends identified through needs assessment, which are derived from hard data relating to objective performance measures.

restraints: Possible limitations on what one might use, do, and deliver. Restraints serve as a type of performance specification.

results: Ends, products, outputs, outcomes—accomplishments and consequences. Usually misses the outputs and outcomes.

soft data: Personal perceptions of results. Soft data is not independently verifiable. While people's perceptions are reality for them, they are not to be relied on without relating to "hard"— independently verifiable—data as well.

strategic alignment: The linking of Mega-, Macro-, and Micro-level planning and results with each other and with Processes and Inputs. By formally deriving what the organization uses, does, produces, and delivers to Mega/external payoffs, strategic alignment is complete.

strategic thinking: Approaching any problem, program, project, activity, or effort by noting that everything that is used, done, produced, and delivered must add value for external clients and society. Strategic thinking starts with Mega.

tactical planning: Finding out what is available to get from What Is to What Should Be at the organizational/Macro level. Tactics are best identified after the overall mission has been selected based on its linkages and contributions to external client and societal (Ideal Vision) results and consequences.

wants: Preferred methods and means assumed to be capable of meeting needs.

What Is: Current operational results and consequences. These could be for an individual, an organization, and/or for society.

What Should Be: Desired or required operational results and consequences. These could be for an individual, an organization, and/or society.

wishes: Desires concerning means and ends. It is important not to confuse *wishes* with *needs.*

Making Sense of Definitions and Their Contribution to a Mega Perspective

Here are some ground rules for strategic thinking and planning:

1. System Approach ≠ Systems Approach ≠ Systematic Approach ≠ Systemic Approach

2. Mega-level Planning ≠ Macro-Level Planning ≠ Micro-Level Planning

3. System Analysis ≠ Systems Analysis

4. Means ≠ Ends

5. Hope ≠ Reality

6. Outcome ≠ Output ≠ Product ≠ Process ≠ Input

7. There are three levels of planning: Mega, Macro, and Micro, and three related types of results: Outcomes, Outputs, Products.

8. Need is a gap in results, not a gap in Process or Input.

9. Needs Assessment ≠ Needs Analysis (nor front-end analysis or problem analysis)

10. Strategic Planning ≠ Tactical Planning ≠ Operational Planning

11. Change Creation ≠ Change Management

Endnote

[1] Based on Kaufman, R., & Watkins, R. (2000, April). Getting serious about results and payoffs: We are what we say, do, and deliver. *Performance Improvement, 39* (4), 23–31.

References

Barker, J. A. (1992). *Future edge: Discovering the new paradigms of success.* New York: William Morrow & Co., Inc.

Barker, J. A. (2001). *The new business of paradigms* (Classic Ed.). St. Paul, MN: Star Thrower Distribution. Videocassette.

Brethower, D. M. (2006). *Defining what to do and why.* Amherst, MA: HRD Press.

Brethower, D. M. (2005, February). Yes we can: A rejoinder to Don Winiecki's rejoinder about saving the world with HPT. *Performance Improvement, 44*(2), 19–24.

Carlton, R. (2006). *Implementation and management of solutions.* Amherst, MA: HRD Press.

Clark, R. E., & Estes, F. (2002). *Turning research into results: A guide to selecting the right performance solutions.* Atlanta, GA: CEP Press.

Davis, I. (2005, May 26). The biggest contract. *The Economist, London, 375*(8428), 87.

Drucker, P. F. (1973). *Management: Tasks, responsibilities, practices.* New York: Harper & Row.

Gerson, R. (2006). *Achieving high performance.* Amherst, MA: HRD Press.

Guerra, I. (2006). *Evaluation and continual improvement of results.* Amherst, MA: HRD Press.

Kaufman, R. A. (1972). *Educational system planning.* Englewood Cliffs, NJ: Prentice-Hall. (Also *Planificacion de systemas educativos* [translation of *Educational system planning*]. Mexico City: Editorial Trillas, S.A., 1973.)

Kaufman, R. (1998). *Strategic thinking: A guide to identifying and solving problems,* Revised Ed. Washington, D.C. & Arlington, VA: The International Society for Performance Improvement and the American Society for Training and Development. (Recipient of the 2001 International Society for Performance Improvement "Outstanding Instructional Communication Award.") Also, Spanish edition, *El pensamiento estrategico.* Centro de Estudios: Roman Areces, S.A., Madrid, Spain.

Kaufman, R. (1999). From how to what to why: The handbook of performance technology as the gateway to the future. In Stolovitch, H., & Keeps, E. *The Handbook of Performance Technology* 2nd Ed. San Francisco, CA: Jossey-Bass.

Kaufman, R. (2000). *Mega planning: Practical tools for organizational success.* Thousand Oaks, CA: Sage Publications.

Kaufman, R. (2002, May/June). What trainers and performance improvement specialists can learn from tragedy: Lessons from September 11, 2001. *Educational Technology.*

Kaufman, R. (2004, October). Mega as the basis for useful planning and thinking. *Performance Improvement. 43*(9), 35–39.

Kaufman, R. (2005, May/June). Choosing success: The rationale for thinking, planning, and doing Mega. *Educational Technology, 45*(2), 59–61.

Kaufman, R. (2006). *30 seconds that can change your life: A decision-making guide for those who refuse to be mediocre.* Amherst, MA: HRD Press.

Kaufman, R., & Bernardez, M. (Eds.) (2005). *Performance Improvement Quarterly, 18*(3).

Kaufman, R., & English, F. W. (1979). *Needs assessment: Concept and application.* Englewood Cliffs, NJ: Educational Technology Publications.

Kaufman, R., & Forbes, R. (2002). Does your organization contribute to society? In the *2002 Team and Organization Development Sourcebook,* pp. 213–224. New York: McGraw-Hill.

Kaufman, R., Guerra, I., & Platt, W. A. (2006). *Practical evaluation for educators: Finding what works and what doesn't.* Thousand Oaks, CA: Corwin Press/Sage.

Kaufman, R., & Keller, J. (1994, Winter) Levels of evaluation: Beyond Kirkpatrick. *Human Resources Quarterly. 5*(4), 371–380.

Kaufman, R., Keller, J., & Watkins, R. (1995). What works and what doesn't: Evaluation beyond Kirkpatrick. *Performance and Instruction. 35*(2), 8–12.

Kaufman, R., & Lick, D. (2000). Mega-level strategic planning: Beyond conventional wisdom. In Boettcher, J., Doyle, M., & Jensen, R. (Eds.). *Technology-driven planning: Principles to practice.* Ann Arbor, MI: Society for College and University Planning.

Kaufman, R., & Lick, D. (2000, November). Change creation and change management: Partners in organizational success. Washington, D.C.: ISPI Culture and Change Conference.

Kaufman, R., & Lick, D. (2000–2001, Winter). Change creation and change management: Partners in human performance improvement. *Performance in practice,* 8–9.

Kaufman, R., & Lick, D. (2004). How to get your organization balanced through change creation (Chapter 30). In Silberman, M., & Phillips, P. (Eds.) *The 2004 Team and Organizational Development Sourcebook,* pp. 255–267. Poughkeepsie, NY: Inkwell Publishing.

Kaufman, R., Oakley-Browne, H., Watkins, R., & Leigh, D. (2003). *Practical strategic planning: Aligning people, performance, and payoffs.* San Francisco, CA: Jossey-Bass/Pfeiffer.

Kaufman, R., & Unger, Z. (2003, August). Evaluation plus: Beyond conventional evaluation. *Performance Improvement, 42*(7), 5–8.

Kaufman, R., Watkins, R., & Leigh, D. (2001). *Useful educational results: Defining, prioritizing, and accomplishing.* Lancaster, PA: Proactive Publishers.

Kaufman, R., Watkins, R., Sims, L., Crispo, N., & Sprague, D. (1997). Costs-consequences analysis. *Performance Improvement Quarterly, 10*(3), 7–21.

Kaufman, R., Watkins, R., Triner, D., & Stith, M. (1998). The changing corporate mind: Organizations, visions, mission, purposes, and indicators on the move toward societal payoffs. *Performance Improvement Quarterly, 11*(3), 32–44.

Lagace, M. (2005, January). How to put meaning back into leading. *Working Knowledge.* Cambridge, MA: Harvard School of Business.

Langdon, D., Whiteside, K., McKenna, M. (1999). *Intervention resource guide: 50 performance improvement tools.* San Francisco, CA: Jossey-Bass.

Leigh, D., Watkins, R., Platt, W., & Kaufman, R. (2000). Alternate models of needs assessment: Selecting the right one for your organization. *Human Resource Development Quarterly, 11*(1), 87–93.

Lick, D., & Kaufman, R. (2000). Change creation: The rest of the planning story. In *Technology-Driven Planning: Principles to Practice.* J. Boettcher, Doyle, M., & Jensen, R., (Eds.). Ann Arbor, MI: Society for College and University Planning.

Mager, R. F. (1997). *Preparing instructional objectives: A critical tool in the development of effective instruction* (3rd Ed.). Atlanta, GA: Center for Effective Performance.

Maslow, A. (1954). *Motivation and personality.* New York: Harper & Row.

Muir, M., Watkins, R., Kaufman, R., & Leigh, D. (1998, April). Costs-consequences analysis: A primer. *Performance Improvement, 37*(4), 8–17, 48.

Peters, T. (1997). *The circle of innovation: You can't shrink your way to greatness.* New York: Knopf.

Peters, T. J., & Waterman, R. H., Jr. (1982). *In search of excellence: Lessons learned from America's best run companies.* New York: Harper & Row.

Popcorn, F. (1991). *The Popcorn report.* New York: Doubleday.

Prahalad, C. K. (2005). *The fortune at the bottom of the pyramid: Eradicating poverty through profits.* Upper Saddle River, NJ: Wharton School Publishing/Pearson Education, Inc.

Roberts, W. (1993). *Victory secrets of Attila the Hun.* New York: Doubleday.

Rummler, G. A. (2004). *Serious performance consulting: According to Rummler.* Silver Spring, MD: International Society for Performance Improvement and the American Society for Training and Development.

Senge, P. M. (1990). *The fifth discipline: The art and practice of the learning organization.* New York: Doubleday-Currency.

Schneider, E. W. (2003, April). Applying human performance technology while staying out of trouble. *Performance Improvement Review, ISPI.*

Stevens, S. S. (1951). Mathematics, measurement, and psychophysics. In Stevens, S. S. *Handbook of Experimental Psychology.* New York: John Wiley & Sons.

Watkins, R. (2006). *Performance by design.* Amherst, MA: HRD Press.

Watkins, R., Leigh, D., Foshay, R., & Kaufman, R. (1998). Kirkpatrick plus: Evaluation and continuous improvement with a community focus. *Educational Technology Research and Development Journal, 46*(4).

Watkins, R., Leigh, D., Kaufman, R. (1999). Choosing a needs assessment model. In Silberman, M. *Team and Organizational Development Sourcebook.* New York: McGraw-Hill.

Watkins, R., Leigh, D., Platt, W., & Kaufman, R. (1998). Needs assessment: A digest, review, and comparison of needs assessment literature. *Performance Improvement, 37*(7), 40–53.

About this Series

Defining and Delivering Successful Professional Practice—HPT in Action

This is the first of Six Books to define and deliver measurable performance improvement. Each volume defines a unique part of a fabric; a fabric to define, develop, implement, and continually improve human and organization performance success. In addition, the series relate to the professional standards in the field.[1]

Why This Series?

Human and Organizational Performance Accomplishment—some call the field HPT (human performance Improvement)—is of great interest to practitioners and clients alike who intend to deliver successful results and payoffs that are based on research, ethics, and solid concepts and tools. Each author provides a practical focus on a unique area, and each book is based on ten principles of professional contribution.

Each book "stands alone" as well as knits with all of the others; together they:

1. Define the field of HPT and Performance Improvement based on the principles of ethical and competent practice,

2. Provide specific guidance on six major areas of professional practice,

3. Are based on a common framework for individual and organizational performance accomplishment, and

4. Reinforce the principles that drive competent and ethical performance improvement.

There is a demand for an integrated approach to Human and Organizational Performance Accomplishment/Human Performance technology. Many excellent books and articles are available (some by the proposed authors) but none cover the entire spectrum of the basic concepts and tools nor do they give the integrated alignment or guidance that each of these six linked books provide.

This series is edited by Roger Kaufman (Ph.D., CPT), Dale Brethower (Ph.D.) and Richard Gerson (Ph.D., CPT).

The six books and the authors are:

Book One: *Change, Choices, and Consequences: A Guide to Mega Thinking and Planning.* Roger Kaufman, Professor Emeritus, Florida State University, Roger Kaufman & Associates, and Distinguished Research Professor, Sonora Institute of Technology

Book 2: *Defining What to Do and Why.* Dale Brethower, Professor Emeritus, Western Michigan University and Research Professor, Sonora Institute of Technology

Book 3: *Performance by Design.* Ryan Watkins, Associate Professor, George Washington University, Senior Research Associate, Roger Kaufman & Associates, and former NSF Fellow

Book 4: *Achieving High Performance.* Richard Gerson, CPT, Ph.D., Gerson Goodson, Inc.

Book 5: *Implementation and Management of Solutions.* Robert Carlton, Senior Partner, Vector Group

Book 6: *Evaluation and Continual Improvement of the Results.* Ingrid Guerra, Ph.D., Assistant Professor, Wayne State University and Associate Research Professor, Sonora Institute of Technology as well as Research Associate, Roger Kaufman & Associates

How This Series Relates to the Professional Performance Improvement Standards

The following table identifies how each book relates to the 10 standards of Performance Technology[2] (identified by numbers in parentheses ( ) pioneered by the International Society for Performance Improvement (ISPI)[3]. In the table on the following page, an "X" identifies coverage and linking and "✓" indicates major focus.

This series, by design, goes beyond these standards by linking everything any organization uses, does, produces, and delivers to adding measurable value to external clients and society. This Six Pack, then, builds on and then goes beyond the current useful criteria and standards in the profession and adds the next dimensions of practical, appropriate, as well as ethical tools, methods, and guidance of what is really required to add value to all of our clients as well as to our shared society.

	Focus on Results (1)	Take a System Approach (2)	Add Value (3)	Partner (4)	Needs Assessment (5)	Performance Analysis (6)	Design to Specification (7)	Selection, Design, & Development (8)	Implementation (9)	Evaluation & Continuous Improvement (10)
Book 1	✓	✓	✓	✓	✓	X	X	X		✓
Book 2	X	✓	✓	X		✓	✓			X
Book 3	X	X	X			✓	✓	✓		X
Book 4	X	X	X	X		✓	X	✓	✓	X
Book 5	X	✓	✓	✓		✓	✓		✓	✓
Book 6	✓	✓	✓	X	✓				X	✓

It all will only be useful to the extent to which this innovative practice becomes standard practice. We invite you to the adventure.

Roger Kaufman, Ph.D., CPT
Dale Brethower, Ph.D.
Richard Gerson, Ph.D., CPT.

Endnotes

1. The Standards of Performance Technology developed by the International Society for Performance Improvement, Silver Spring, Maryland.

2. Slightly modified.

3. Another approach to standardization of performance are a set of competencies developed by the American Society for Training and Development (ASTD) which are more related to on-the-job performance.

About the Author

Roger Kaufman, Ph.D. (New York University) is professor emeritus, Florida State University, Director of Roger Kaufman & Associates, and Distinguished Research Professor at the Sonora Institute of Technology (Mexico). He is a past president, member for life and Thomas Gilbert Award winner, all with the International Society for Performance Improvement (ISPI, and is the recipient of ASTD's Distinguished Contribution to Workplace Learning and Performance award. He is a certified performance technologist (ISPI) and a diplomate in Educational Psychology of the American Psychological Association. Kaufman has published 38 books and over 245 articles on strategic planning, performance improvement, quality management and continuous improvement, needs assessment, management, and evaluation.